IF I'M FORGIVEN,
WHY DO I STILL FEEL GUILTY?

If I'm Forgiven, Why Do I Still Feel Guilty?

BERNARD BANGLEY

Harold Shaw Publishers
Wheaton, Illinois

ISBN 0-87788-397-1

Cover design by Ron Kadrmas

Library of Congress Cataloging-in-Publication Data

Bangley, Bernard, 1935–
    If I'm forgiven, why do I still feel guilty? / Bernard Bangley.
      p.   cm.
    Rev. ed. of: Forgiving yourself. ©1986.
    Includes bibliographical references.
    ISBN 0-87788-397-1
    1. Forgiveness of sin. 2. Forgiveness—Religious aspects—
Christianity. 3. Guilt—Religious aspects—Christianity. I. Bangley,
Bernard, 1935–   Forgiving yourself. II. Title.
III. Title: If I am forgiven, why do I still feel guilty?
BT795.B293   1992
234'.5—dc20
                                   91-44751
                                   CIP

---

99 98 97 96 95

10 9 8 7 6 5 4 3 2

Contents

Contents

Introduction

Easier Said than Done

A bad conscience embitters the sweetest comforts; a good one sweetens the bitterest crosses.
Anonymous

She came to me from many miles away. In less than thirty years she had managed to fill her life with incredible complications. The young woman in tears before me was a living example that selfish choices are not often good choices. She had thought she was seeking happiness when she left her wealthy but un-communicative husband. Moving in with her sym-pathetic friend seemed to relieve many tensions.

For more than a year, her exchange of luxury for simple, trusting friendship was a pleasant interlude. But now, for a variety of reasons, she wanted to return to her husband. Her friend was under-standing, but his very kindness became a source of pain for her. She knew she had been using him without any consideration for the natural emotional attachments that would develop. Furthermore, she felt that she had been using everyone in her life. Her burden of guilt was overwhelming. An hour of weeping and talking about it with me was far from enough to help her.

I will never forget the pleading despair in her swollen eyes when she asked me, "What do you tell people about forgiving themselves?"

All I could answer at the time was, "It's not easy." But her question lingered with me. I thought of the many people I have met in my experience as pastor who share her problem. The particulars are different with each individual, but the basic snag is the same. *If I'm forgiven, why do I still feel guilty?*

Many modern Christians are not fully aware of what the Bible teaches regarding forgiveness. Some think they know all the answers. They are attempting to teach others while carrying around a load as heavy as Christian's in *The Pilgrim's Progress*. Others do not regularly participate in the life of the church. Some who seek help here have no religious viewpoint at all. Whoever you are, you will bring to these pages your own special kind of baggage.

Perhaps you have discovered that friends aren't much help. They really don't understand you. The answers they give are too easy. They become impatient with you. They remind you how many people are worse off than you are. "Snap out of it," they say. They honestly expect you to do that for them. It's like the movie scriptwriter's cure for hysteria—slap her in the face, and when she regains her composure, kiss her. That's not the way it works in the world we live in. Neither will the instant prayers of your friends pull you out of your guilt, no matter how much they urge the love of God upon you.

You will be told, "Time heals. All you have to do is be heroic, maybe take some pills for a while. Sooner or later you will forget about it. Keep your chin up! Smile! Time will take care of it."

But time heals nothing. Time can even be your enemy. It will let the negative influences of feeling guilty work greater and greater destruction in your body and soul. Time may push it deeper so that you are less aware of it, but it is still there. It will come rushing back into your awareness by the slightest suggestion.

So how can a book be better than a friend? Only in one way. There is no emotional involvement here. I don't know you and you don't know me. The way you feel right now will not affect my appetite. You can't play your little games of self-pity on me. If what you read stings because I have hit the nail on the head, you can't tell me I am unkind. A book doesn't have to be careful about what it says in order to protect your feelings. You can be alone with these pages, unconcerned about the revelations of your facial expressions or the messages of body language. If you are helped, even in a small way, you owe me nothing.

The only way I can be helpful to you is if you understand me. Therefore, I shall write simply—just as though we were sitting down for a conversation together. I will avoid all technical jargon. I will offer no easy answers to difficult questions. I will refuse to play those little religious games that are all too common in literature such as this. I won't pretend that a single verse of Scripture will solve all your problems. I present no false hope that your life will be straightened out the instant you finish reading this.

What I will do is gently guide you through a process of recognition that will help you identify your problem. Then we can see what the Bible teaches that is relevant to the question, and look at some practical steps toward recovery.

The Magnitude of the Problem

The fact is, feeling forgiven is a tremendous hurdle in life. A few pathological personalities, I am told, hurt people and steal things without feeling any pangs of conscience. That may be. But such people are rare. Most of us pay a heavy penalty. The hardened criminal, the cynical business leader, the tough bully, the cool politician, and the uncaring parent all exhibit those telltale twitches on a polygraph that point to a morality beneath their masquerading exteriors. There is a seed of human decency planted in each one of us, an innate knowledge of right and wrong as clear as the Ten Commandments. We can deny it. Our culture can set its own make-believe standards, but the guilt response is universal. It almost seems to be programmed into our genes.

Some of us are more susceptible than others. A few of us are too highly sensitive. As a general rule, extremes are unhealthy. If you think you are absolutely insensitive to the feelings of others, or if, on the other hand, you are emotionally distraught to the point of being incapacitated, you need more help than I am going to be able to give you in these brief pages. I urge you to seek competent counseling.

If, on the other hand, you are among those who have made some mistakes and know it, who believe in a forgiving heavenly Father, and yet still can't seem to put it all behind and start afresh, welcome to the club! You have far more company than you imagine. I can even say, "I know how you feel." I can't say that to a person going blind. Or to someone who has lost a spouse or watched a child die. I can't say that to an amputee or to a victim of a poor investment. But I can honestly identify with anyone who has been wrestling with lingering, haunting guilt. I have known what it is to play scenes through my imagination, asking, "What if?" I have wondered long and hard what would have happened with my family if I had not packed our belongings into a moving van. I have seen how my choices along the way set up the possibilities for disasters great and small. I have watched with horror when the slightest suggestion from my lips created a chain of events that I was helpless to stop.

Such experiences are cumulative. Unless we learn to forgive ourselves, they will catch up with us. Nagging guilt has sent many people to the doctor. Sometimes the complaint is vague. The best the physician can offer is a placebo or a tranquilizer. At other times the illness is quite specific and beyond debate. It can be easily measured on an EKG. Our emotional system can open doors to infections that are ordinarily closed. Our feelings can create organic disturbances in our bodies. The circulatory and digestive systems are particularly vulnerable. These are not imaginary illnesses. Genuine damage is being done to living tissue. Although the blows are not physical, they are blows no less.

The book of Proverbs makes this sweeping statement: "As he thinketh in his heart, so is he" (Proverbs 23:7, KJV). Your emotions will affect your behavior. Bruce Hutchison, a practicing clinical psychologist, sees this kind of thing every day. "Beneath the level of your ordinary awareness is a pervasive emotional logic that constantly influences what you do, why you do it, and how well you carry it out. It affects how your marriage works, how you raise your children, what you expect from relationships, how you get along with your boss, how much income you settle for, your habitual state of tension, your physical well-being, your sexual satisfaction, what you're searching for in life, how much fun you have, and how satisfied you are with yourself. In other words, it affects everything."[1]

Guilt will also eat away at your nerves. It will make you "jumpy." There will be no peace for you if you are ashamed of yourself and live in terror that others might discover the truth. Does your heart skip a beat when the telephone rings? Are you terrified by a knock at your door? Do you hesitate to open a letter? Are you being robbed of precious sleep? Does a good meal taste like pine bark? Such things are only the beginning of what can happen if you ignore your responsibility to yourself.

The ultimate penalty is spiritual. An escapee from prison hides from policemen. A student who is not prepared to answer looks away from the teacher. A child who has misbehaved sulks in a corner. The person who feels unforgiven will naturally avoid God. The ancient story in Genesis tells us that when Adam and Eve disobeyed God and ate the forbidden fruit, they tried to hide from him.

Unfortunately, this is standard textbook behavior. We are turning away from our one source of help. The doctor in Lady Macbeth's famous sleepwalking scene puts his finger squarely on it: "This disease is beyond my practice . . . Infected minds to their deaf pillows will discharge their secrets. More needs she the divine than the physician. God, God forgive us all!"

The United States Treasury keeps something called a "conscience fund." It started in 1811 when someone anonymously sent five dollars to ease his mind. William Simon, a former secretary of the treasury, told Ann Landers he had never heard of it. But a little investigation uncovered the quiet fact that it does exist. And it has grown dramatically since James Madison was president. The largest anonymous contribution ($125,990.48) was received in 1980. The total in the fund at the present time is about five million dollars.

Most of the contributions come with a letter of explanation: "This money order for $90 is to reimburse the government for the time I spent on the phone with a certain relative who called me a lot." Or how about this one: "Here's $6,000 I owe for back taxes. I haven't been able to sleep nights. If I still can't sleep, I'll send you the rest."

The important thing is that something be done to relieve us. Once we have accepted God's forgiveness, we still need to forgive ourselves. It is not easy. Not for me. Not for you. But it can be done. Let's see how.

Who can say, "I have kept my heart pure; I am clean and without sin"?
Proverbs 20:9

Let It Hit Home

☐ What effects has nagging guilt had in your life? Health problems? Avoidance of people? Sleepless nights?

☐ How long have you struggled with guilt—to the extent that you were aware it was a guilt problem?

PART ONE

Our Human Tendencies

1

Denial Is Not Confession

Before God can deliver us we must undeceive ourselves.
St. Augustine

The First Step—Confession

Too bad it is such a difficult step. We have a built-in resistance to admitting a personal failure, accepting a personal responsibility, or shouldering guilt.

Imagine this exchange: Someone is talking with a friend about the new car he recently purchased. Best deal he's ever made! He got a good trade-in; the salesman was a friend of his cousin. Runs like a top. No mechanic has ever put a wrench to it. Gas mileage is terrific. "I really made a smart move when I bought this beaut!"

But the friend does not respond with similar enthusiasm. He points out to the new car owner that he might have gotten a better deal if he had shopped elsewhere before he traded. He also tells him he just read an article that proved another kind of car had superior engineering. "And, by the way, the book value of your old car was higher than what they allowed you."

Have you ever in your life heard one conversation in which the new owner agreed with the other person? Can you imagine him agreeing that he had been taken in and was not such a smart bargainer after all? No way! Not even if the new car were in a garage at that very moment running up a five-hundred-dollar repair bill for the seventh time! In fact, he won't admit any such thing until it's trading time again, and he's ready to make the next best deal of his life.

Recognizing Denial

Who can say it? "I made a mistake." "I sinned."

It was King Herod's unwillingness to admit his blunder that cost John the Baptist his head. Herod had arrested John because of the nasty things he was saying about his marriage to his brother's wife, Herodias. The lady wanted him killed, but Herod was afraid of the "holy man" and would only imprison him.

The New Testament tells us that when King Herod gave a birthday party for himself, he invited all his courtiers and officers and the leading citizens of Galilee. For a little entertainment he encouraged his stepdaughter, Salome, to dance. She was a smash hit. The king, overcome with pleasure, said to her, "I will give you anything you ask, up to half my kingdom!" Salome consulted with her mother and returned to ask Herod for John the Baptist's head.

The king was greatly troubled. But because of his public promises he felt he had to keep his word. In despair, he sent a guard with orders to bring John's head to Salome. He didn't want to do it. But he didn't want to look like a doting fool either. All of these important people were watching him, enjoying his dilemma, curious to see how he would wriggle out of this one. Think of the courage it would have taken to blush and say, "I'm sorry. I've been a silly old man. My enthusiasm for this young girl distorted my judgment. I can see now that they took me for a stupid old fool, and I have not disappointed them. I made a mistake when I made that vow." He couldn't do it. Could you?

And yet there is no shame in admitting that you have been wrong. It's only another way of saying that you are wiser now than you were then.

So why the hangup? What makes it so much easier to deny than to confess?

Society's Lessons

The little card from my auto insurance company advises, "If you are involved in an accident, do not admit responsibility." Corporations and individuals are cautioned by attorneys to make no statements in public or private that might be used as ammunition later. In short, the first step on the way to spiritual health feels like an illness! It goes against every survival skill we have learned.

Denial comes as naturally as breathing and we are often unconscious of what we are doing. Dr. Kubler-Ross identifies denial as the first response to a doctor's report that we have a terminal illness. "I feel too well." "It can't be." "The laboratory made a mistake." An alcoholic plays the same game. "I can control myself." "I am not addicted to drink." "I don't need any help."

Investigating this phenomenon, I watched twenty episodes of "Peoples' Court." The drama is played out in the sanitized environment of Judge Wapner's television studio, but it is one of the few slices of real life that can be seen on TV. The characters and the situations are not fictional. Some of the contests are "stranger than fiction." The arguments center around neighbors' pets, hair dressers' mistakes, poor limousine service, troublesome roommates, and botched services of all kinds.

In the course of a month I saw a total of thirty-eight pairs of argumentative litigants. A post-verdict interview is conducted after most of the cases are heard. Without exception, every loser denied making any kind of mistake or being at fault. "The judge didn't give me a chance to tell him everything." "I heard what he said, but I know I'm right." "There is no justice."

Big-time criminals deny any guilt by appealing the court's decision as far up the ladder toward the Supreme Court as they can. In jail, many wonder why they are there. Frederick the Great visited a prison in Potsdam. Each prisoner he met assured him that he was innocent, the victim of a miscarriage of justice. When one man looked down at the floor and said, "Your majesty, I am guilty and I deserve this punishment," the monarch called the warden. "Free this rascal and get him out of our prison," he ordered, "before he corrupts all the innocoent people in here!" More than a century ago Soren Kierkegaard pointed out that it is easy enough to agree with the general statement, "All have sinned." But the particular application, "I have sinned," sticks somewhere between our heart and our brain.

Try to imagine a delegate to the United Nations, having heard the charges against his country's behavior, bowing his head and saying, "We did it. I'm sorry!" Wouldn't that be refreshing? I have lived enough years now to be able to interpret political denials. When charges are dismissed as "lies," there is some substance to them. If the speaker is angry and calls them "damned lies!" they are probably true.

It is impossible to overstate how pervasive denial is in our culture. Even elementary school children have learned the art. "I didn't do anything!" is a phrase often heard by parents and authorities.

Now it may be that denial is sometimes in your best interest. It may save you a dollar or spare you punishment. But we are considering a matter that is entirely personal. Forgiving yourself is, frankly, a spiritual problem. Denial here is entirely negative. There will be no healing of your soul until the matter is confessed.

How to Avoid Confession

Human psychology provides us with an arsenal of weapons with which to defend ourselves against anxiety. Often they come into service automatically. We make no conscious decision about them. We may repress the memory of some mortifying personal experience. We may become fanatical crusaders, denouncing the very thing we desire. We may rationalize, giving good reasons to justify our conduct. Spend a day with a highway patrolman and listen to the excuses for speeding. The taxpayer mentioned in the first chapter might well have concluded that the government would waste his money, and that cheating was commonplace—even expected.

A popular method of avoiding confession is projection—blaming someone else. The clarinetist who squeaks in a concert blames it on the reed. A hostile person feels as though he were the recipient of hostility. Often parents are blamed for a young person's poor choices, or for creating an environment that fosters criminal behavior. Edward Fitzgerald's *Rubáiyát of Omar Khayyám* projects all the blame to God himself:

> Oh, Thou, who Man of baser Earth didst make,
> And who with Eden didst devise the Snake;
> For all the Sin wherewith the Face of Man
> Is blacken'd, Man's Forgiveness give—and take!

Here it is in simple translation:

God: Adam, who told you you were naked? Have you been eating what I told you not to eat?
Adam: That woman you gave me picked the fruit and made me eat it. It's her fault; not mine!
God: Eve, what is this thing you have done?
Eve: Now listen, Lord. The snake over there put me up to it. You created the snake, so it's all your fault!

In chapter six we will see how the experiences we have at home while growing up can influence our feelings of guilt. The legacy of dysfunctional families is clearly observable in adults. But sometimes we are not justified in shifting blame for our faults from ourselves to our parents. We accuse Mom and Dad while we excuse ourselves. "Of course I'm fat! Mother always made me clean my plate. She taught me to like greasy food. When I was a child she stuffed me with buttered biscuits." Here is nothing but ordinary denial by projection. You can't point one finger at someone else without pointing three at yourself. Remind yourself that you make mistakes; mistakes don't make you.

It is also quite common today to insulate ourselves from contradictions. We deal with highly charged emotional issues by reducing them to intellectual terms. We invent new names for old sins. Laziness becomes "goofing off." We no longer hear debates about the difference between fornication and adultery. The misuse of sex now has a long catalog of safe, new terminology. A skunk by any other name would smell the same, but in genteel western Virginia society, "polecat" is more acceptable.

Bureaucrats and public relations specialists are expert at this. A military general can speak for hours about thermonuclear war. He will never use a word that produces images of slaughter and death. There will be no fire, no blood, no devastation of homes. Instead, he will substitute an assortment of euphemisms and slide-rule jargon. He will speak of "overpressures," "blast parameters," "temperature thresholds," and "fallout interfaces." This is a subtle mental game that is also a form of denial.

Enthusiastic Christians easily fall prey to this. Instead of saying, "I thought," they say, "The Lord told me." God gets blamed for a lot of second- and third-rate ideas. Some of the newly converted are eager to view their entire life experience as a ministry to God. This leads them to explain that Christ is the motivating force behind everything they do.

Some years ago Judi Culbertson and Patti Bard brought out an irreverent little book called *Games Christians Play*. It contains a sparkling chapter on how to write "Christian" letters. Here are a couple of their rules:

Do not say: "The mission board rejected me as a candidate because I flunked the preliminary qualification tests."

Do say: "Despite much labor, love, prayer and plans, the Lord has, in His infinite wisdom, seen fit to close the door to the mission field . . ."

Do not say: "We bought a new candy-apple red Mustang last Thursday. Wowie!"

Do say: "A week and three days ago, God in His mercy provided us with a small automobile which we hope and trust will be used greatly in the service of picking up and discharging the neighborhood children to and from Sunday School."[2]

Soon after I first read that book I received a letter from some dedicated Christians who said almost the same thing in all seriousness.

If you seek forgiveness for yourself, avoid this trap. Call a spade a spade. Rattlesnake venom becomes no less deadly if you call it "snake juice" or "vitreous herpetological toxin."

There is also a shoulder-shrugging kind of admission of truth that falls short of genuine, healthy confession. It acknowledges facts while dismissing all accompanying problems.

Here is an interesting real-life example of how differently people can respond when involved in scandal. In the summer of 1983 the House of Representatives censured two congressmen for having sexual relations with teenage pages. One of them was described as "very stoic, very tough. He doesn't crumble or crack at all."[3] The congressman's public statement included these words:

"In my statement last Thursday on the floor of the House, I admitted to a very serious error in judgment ten years ago, and said I would not contest the procedure recommended to the House by the Committee on Standards of Official Conduct. I vigorously reaffirm today the full text of that statement.

"All members of Congress are in need of humbling experiences from time to time. But I have never been made so aware of the capacity for decency and strength of the American people as I have been in contemplating the reaction of my constituents to the events of the past week. Their friendship and trust have strengthened me, and have, I hope, helped me to emerge from the present situation a wiser, a more tolerant and more complete human being." [4]

The other congressman exhibited sharply contrasting behavior. In a state of emotional turmoil, he turned and faced the House directly when Speaker Thomas O'Neill read the censure resolution. The man expressed himself in these words:

"Mr. Speaker, this is one of the most difficult moments in my life, and it has been an unparalleled ordeal for my family.

"We pay for our sins in life, and in making my peace I take comfort that our Lord promised me forgiveness seventy times seven. It is less easy for us to forgive ourselves or our brothers, but I have asked for and received the forgiveness of those I hurt most, my wife and family.

"I have asked my friends and neighbors to forgive me as well. But Mr. Speaker, I have not yet apologized to my colleagues in this body for the shame I have brought down on this institution . . . I want the members to know that I am sorry and that I apologize to one and all."[5]

This is the place to start. Admit it. All else comes later. Until you get over this hurdle, you have not started the race. Until you open this door, the fresh air and sunshine that await you will be locked out.

Conclusion

Denial, in any form, is not confession. Seneca, the Roman who lived about the same time as Christ, put it quite bluntly: "Why does no one confess his vices? Because he is still in them! It is the one who wakes that reports the dream."

It is confession that starts the process of forgiving yourself. There is no substitute, no alternative. Confession is the first thing that is required whether your fall is great or small, whether it is a spiritual calamity or a simple mission of a personal goal. Go ahead. Admit it. It is a healthy, healing thing to drop all evasions and say that you have failed, sinned, blundered, hurt someone, disappointed yourself.

Now how do you do that? We have considered what confession is not. Let's look at what it is.

> If we claim to be without sin, we deceive ourselves and the truth is not in us. If we confess our sins, he is faithful and just and will forgive us our sins and purify us from all unrighteousness. If we claim we have not sinned, we make him out to be a liar and his word has no place in our lives.
> *1 John 1:8-10*

Let It Hit Home

☐ What clues serve to let you know that you are "in denial"? (If you're not sure, ask a friend or family member how they know when you are in denial.)

☐ What kind of "double-talk" (words that disguise the real meaning) are you most guilty of?

2

Good for the Soul

When the soul has laid down its faults at the feet of God, it feels as though it had wings.
Eugenie de Guerin

Most of us have filed away a significant collection of troublesome secrets. There is no account book more accurate than your mind. Human memory is incredible. We say we have "forgotten" something, but it is still there, stored for life. It is only buried out of sight.

It has often been said that confession is good for the soul. It's a way to clean out your mental file. It works like a ditch that drains a stagnant pond, a vent that exchanges air. Confession is a pressure-relieving valve you can turn.

What images do you get when you hear the word confession? Do you picture someone in handcuffs giving the details of a crime? Perhaps you think of an ornate closet in a dark corner of a sanctuary, with a priest on the other side of a curtain. Or maybe you see a husband explaining the lipstick on his collar. When a term like this is used, it is important that we share the same definition.

Confession is an idea rooted in the Bible. In order to understand it we must come to terms with a word that often accompanies it. The two words go together, like tractor and trailer. The other word is *sin*, the thing confessed.

A Biblical Definition of Sin

The world has difficulty deciding what needs to be classified as sin. There are too many conflicting catalogs. What is taboo for one group of people is no problem at all for another. Whether your behavior will be praised or condemned often depends upon where and when you happen to live!

The confusion of sin by a multitude of detailed regulations reached its zenith in the time of Christ. When you read in the Gospels that Jesus criticized the scribes and the Pharisees, you are reading about an explosive confrontation of healthy religion with diseased religion.

For Jesus' fellow Jews, nothing was more sacred, more absolute, and more final than the Law. A summary of the Law of God is contained in the Ten Commandments. Sin is:

1. Worshiping false gods.
2. Making idols.
3. Misusing God's name.
4. Working on the Sabbath day.
5. Not honoring one's parents.
6. Murder.
7. Adultery.
8. Stealing.

9. Giving false evidence.
10. Wanting what belongs to another.

An amplification of these ten basic principles is mixed in with the faith-history of the first five books of the Bible (called the Pentateuch). These books, from Genesis to Deuteronomy, are still referred to as "The Law."

The scribes of Jesus' day had continued the process of deducing particular applications for these great moral principles. They had an answer for almost any question. Perhaps it is better to say they had a regulation for almost any behavior. This is what was known in New Testament times as "the tradition of the elders" (Matthew 15:2, KJV). It was oral law, as opposed to written law. The scribes made a business of memorizing it and passing it on. They were the legal experts. These ideas, accumulated generation after generation, were eventually written down in a thick volume known as the *Mishnah.*

The Pharisees made it their business to live by the Law as expounded by the scribes. Since this law wasn't universally practiced, it gave them a certain elitist pride. The Pharisees considered everyone else "sinners" and went out of their way to avoid them.

Jesus was a religious amateur from their point of view. He was without proper training and credentials. They watched with shocked horror as he disregarded details of the Law on numerous occasions. They could not abide his familiarity with "sinners." They constricted the love of God; Jesus expanded it.

Legalistic religion has always had tremendous popular appeal. It is very comforting to think that one has pleased God by performing certain duties and abstaining from certain behavior. If you already have all the answers to any question worth asking, you won't be bothered by questions you can't answer. There is something inherently safe in being a Pharisee.

This popular, moralistic religion is one of good works. It springs from the notion that God will love us if we are good and reject us if we are bad. How many of us were made to feel that our own parents conditioned their love this way? If we fulfilled their hopes and dreams, married the right person, brought home a Little League trophy, played the first-chair trombone, or got accepted by the right college—then we would be their darling. But only then. It can come as a shock that God does not deal with us that way.

Poor Martin Luther! He tried so hard. Plagued with guilt, he tried to find relief in mortification of the flesh and penances of every kind. He ultimately discovered that salvation is a free gift of God's grace—he could never earn it with ten lifetimes of good works. Paul Tournier has pointed out that Luther's cry of relief is what we call the Reformation. The cost of our salvation was paid by God. We owe him no bills. And yet, a pietistic expression of faith has returned to the very churches that were born in the Reformation. "Moralism has re-established the idea of merit, of a grace which is conditional. And in some Protestant circles these conditions so proliferate and harden down as to be oppressive."[6]

It is highly probable that you are feeling guilty for some things that are unimportant to the Almighty. The preacher may shake his finger and his Bible at you for the wrong reasons. But there is no doubt that you are a sinner. We all are. We need a mature under-standing of what is meant by the term *sinner.* It means we can't draw a line between good people and bad people. We are all in the same boat. Our natural tendency is to move away from God and do what is evil in his sight.

The message of the Bible is that our very natures are warped. We are "fallen" creatures. Even the most God-fearing, teetotaling, public-praying pietist you can find is one of us. A sinner. And this sin will find expression in many individual ways. It is a trick of self-deception that the self-righteous never place their particular sin on the list! Pride, for instance. Christ was hard on that one. Read what he said about the two men who went to the temple to pray. Gossip. That's another bad one. Paul puts it right there among the worst in the first chapter of Romans.

An interesting thing about the biblical idea of sin is that it is always done *against God.* You may have hurt another person or been a menace to society, but it doesn't stop there. The offended party is always God. A classic expression of this is the fifty-first psalm. King David, after his affair with Bathsheba, says: "Have mercy on me, O God . . . Wash away all my iniquity and cleanse me from my sin. . . . Against you, you only, have I sinned and done what is evil in your sight . . ." (Psalm 51:1-4).

The Importance of Confession to God of Our Sins

The ancient law stated: "When anyone is guilty in any of these ways, he must confess in what way he has sinned and, as a penalty for the sin he has committed, he must bring to the LORD a female lamb or goat from the flock as a sin offering . . ." (Leviticus 5:5).

Ezra is described as praying and confessing, "weeping and throwing himself down before the house of God" (Ezra 10:1). Daniel wrote, "I prayed to the Lord my God and confessed . . ." (Daniel 9:4).

Other psalms join the fifty-first in an act of confession. A good example is the thirty-second. "I acknowledged my sin to you and did not cover up my iniquity. I said, 'I will confess my transgressions to the LORD'—and you forgave the guilt of my sin" (Psalm 32:5, KJV).

The New Testament continues this emphasis upon the importance of confession. When John baptized people in the Jordan River they confessed their sins (Mark 1:5). The First Epistle of John makes this strong assertion: "If we confess our sins, he is faithful and just and will forgive us our sins and purify us from all unrighteousness" (1 John 1:9).

Jesus, time and again, dealt with individual sinners with a special kind of compassion. People seemed to know that they could freely approach him with their problems. One beautiful exchange was between Jesus and the Samaritan woman at the well (John 4:5-42). This, too, is confession.

How You Can Confess Today

If you have grown up in a religious environment, there are probably some formal avenues of confession already known to you. For Roman Catholics, confession is sacramental. It is expected at least annually. Now called the Sacrament of Reconciliation, it may take place either in the traditional curtained confessional or in face-to-face conversations with a priest.

Protestants are heirs to a tradition that is suspicious of formal, required confession. Yet even when reformers pointed out the difficulties involved in this issue nearly five hundred years ago, they continued to insist on the importance of its practice. John Calvin said that it was vital and could never be disapproved. What he sought was "secret confession which is made to God . . . followed by voluntary confession to men."[7] The result of this tradition is that most Protestants, unfortunately, tend to confine their personal confession to a moment of conversion. Pastoral counseling provides an opportunity for such expression, but it touches only a small percentage of a congregation.

Jews are familiar with a period of penitence during High Holy Days. The emphasis is always communal. One prays for the forgiveness of "our" sins. An individual is free to approach God directly in silent prayer, with no rabbi involved. In rare instances a rabbi may hear a deathbed confession *(Vidui)*.

Regardless of your background, now is a good time to look creatively at the possibilities open to you for confession. The easiest way to get something "off your chest" is simply to tell another person. But be careful! Not everyone is a desirable confessor. It is usually a mistake for an unfaithful partner in love or business to unload the distressing facts without some very good preparation. Irreparable damage can be done to the relationship.

Sometimes the burden is merely shifted from one person to another, and that is seldom healing. Actually, confession of this sort intends, whether consciously or unconsciously, to hurt the offended party.

Some things are best kept secret from some people forever. There are other ways, as we will see later, of making it up to that person without revealing all the gory details.

Many seek out a close friend at such a moment. Genuine friends can be a real help. If they are honestly sympathetic, if they can be trusted to keep what you divulge in confidence, if they are not possessive in their relationship with you, then you may have everything you need in that close friend. But if you are feeding some weakness in the other person's own personality with your problem, trouble lies ahead. Such a person will seem to be all support while doing everything possible to make matters worse for you. It is not uncommon for a friend to develop sexual attraction while listening to your tale of woe. For others, knowledge of your problem is either "too good to keep" or "not worth keeping." Tell a trusted friend, if you have one. But be careful.

This brings us back to the professionals. Counselors of varied descriptions and credentials are available for a fee and assure you the privacy of professional confidence. Sometimes an appointment at a physician's office becomes a time of confession. Many doctors have discovered that talking-it-out sessions are an important part of curing an illness. Quite frankly, they also hear quite a number of confessions in the process of surgery—much of it involuntary. One reason some people have a fear of anesthesia is that they know they may lose control and "spill the beans" in a state of semiconsciousness.

Clergy, of course, have fulfilled the traditional role in society as confessor. There is something especially valuable in confessing to someone recognized as a representative of God. We have observed the biblical view that when we wrong another person (or even ourselves), God is the one we have actually sinned against. So God certainly needs to be in on the confession.

Like friends, priests, pastors, rabbis, and chaplains come in varying degrees of competency and trustworthiness. In most communities, there is usually one such religious professional who has a reputation for being a good listener. The denominational brand name is unimportant. Try to find such a person. Look for one who is compassionate, warmly human and loving, not judgmental and narrow. If you do, you will have found someone like Christ.

But suppose you can't find an ordained person who fits that description. Or maybe there are some things you honestly don't want your pastor to know, in spite of the generosity of his spirit. Today there is a growing fellowship of people within the Christian church who are recovering the New Testament way of supporting each other emotionally. If you look in the right place you are likely to discover a community of Christians from all walks of life who will give you the acceptance and understanding you need. Again, take caution. Such groups may be neurotic. They may use all the correct language and be all smiles and hugs. At the same time they can be a source of narrow judgment, ridicule, gossip, and subtle pressures you don't need. Take your time. Don't take such a group or any of its members into your confidence until you have honestly gotten to know them and feel yourself to be a part of them. If you happen to stumble upon the real thing, thank God for your blessing and go ahead and unburden yourself. If you find help, it becomes your responsibility to help another.

There is yet another way. Private confession is not only possible, but also highly desirable. The matter is between you and God. Tell God about it. You need no human intercessor. Learn to pray. In the privacy of your room or office, unburden your soul to God. Get it out. Write God a letter. Put it all right there on paper. Even the nastiest details. Sign it. Then, if you want, burn or shred it. In any event, the rottenness has been externalized. Now that it is out in the open, you can face it. In the presence of your heavenly Father, you can confess the thing, stop pretending, and then start thinking and feeling like one of God's creatures again. You will praise the day this happens for you.

As a young man I heard an angry preacher decry the Christian church's treasury of formal prayers. He said they were "dead prayers embalmed in print." That was catchy. I rather liked it, even though I did not share his vehemence.

And then I heard the late Gert Behanna. She gave a powerful testimony about her empty, secular life. She took us through a satin-lined world of luxury and alcoholism, of broken relationships and attempted suicide. She told of the day she attended her first service at an Episcopal church. Then she quoted the classic prayer of confession from memory for us:

Almighty and most merciful Father,
we have erred and strayed from thy ways like lost
  sheep,
we have followed too much the devices and desires
  of our own hearts,
we have offended against thy holy laws,

we have left undone those things which we ought to
have done,
and we have done those things which we ought not
to have done.
But thou, O Lord, have mercy upon us,
spare thou those who confess their faults,
restore thou those who are penitent,
according to thy promises declared unto mankind
in Christ Jesus our Lord;
and grant, O most merciful Father, for his sake,
that we may hereafter live a godly, righteous, and
sober life,
to the glory of thy holy name. Amen.[8]

Believe me when I tell you. That prayer lived. For
Gert. For us. It can live for you.

Create in me a clean heart, O God,
and put a new and right spirit within me.
Psalm 51:10, RSV

Let It Hit Home

❒ What first comes to your mind when you hear the word "sin"?

❒ When was the last time you confessed to another person? If you have never confessed to a person, when was the last time you made specific confession to God?

PART TWO

The Nature
of God

3

God As Friend

---

*Nothing in this lost and ruined world bears
the meek impress of the Son of God so
surely as forgiveness.*
Alice Cary

God is your friend. Let that sink in.

God loves you. God cares. God is hurt when you are hurt, happy when you are happy. God desires nothing for you but the best.

Do you believe it?

Probably not. Let's be honest. If you think about God at all it is likely not as friend. Judge, maybe. Stern Lawgiver. Demanding Parent. Critical Overseer. It is amazing how readily we picture the Almighty as an enemy—someone out to get us.

Let anything bad happen and guess whose will it is? Ask an insurance agent to define an "act of God." You will be told: earthquakes, tornadoes, hurricanes, volcanic eruptions, floods, drought, pestilence, plague, and famine. Even war, as manmade a disaster as you will ever find, is often blamed on God.

If I were God, I would be put out with that kind of thinking. I would say, "Hey, wait a minute! Do you think I prefer death to life? Is my joy in that which is decaying, putrid, and sickly? Do I desire to transform my living world into one that is dead? How can you imagine that I derive some sort of necrophilic pleasure in destroying for the sake of destruction? In my creation, decay produces new life; change means re-creation. Don't think of me as a petulant, destructive child knocking over blocks in a playroom."

The concept of God as an enemy springs from our own feelings of guilt. If God were looking for good reasons to punish us, we know he would find plenty. Like the thief on the cross, we could say, "We are getting what our deeds deserve" (Luke 23:41). We can think of perfectly justifiable grounds for being punished. When we have confessed and feel forgiven again, our attitude toward the Almighty will change dramatically.

For every person who thinks of God as an enemy, there are probably three who see only divine indifference. They can't imagine that God even notices, let alone cares.

Many of us are willing to agree that some kind of intelligence is responsible for the creation of our intricate and beautiful world. It seems too orderly to be an accident. But many modern people, like the deists of Thomas Jefferson's day, deny any possibility that such a Creator could remain actively involved in history. They see God as a watchmaker who puts it all together, starts it ticking, and then has no further interest in it. God is neither friend nor enemy. He is aloof, looking the other way, too busy being God.

Anyway, caring can hurt. It costs. It involves anxiety and sweat. Surely God must be above such things, existing in eternal serenity the way the ancient Epicureans imagined. If God were to accept the burden of love or permit himself to feel pity, he would never be able to relax! In order to be God, he must be coolly indifferent.

What We Think God Is Like

Of course, people hold many other concepts of God. Some view him as an interested spectator, cheering from the sidelines. Others keep him distanced from personal involvement by focusing on his holiness. The Old Testament encourages this. Isaiah reminds us twenty-nine times that God is "The Holy One." The Hebrew word for "holy" (qadosh) elementally means "apart, separate, different." This absolute "otherness" is a sharp dividing line between a holy God and sinful humans. It is a grand concept with many advantages. For me, it is superior to the palsy-walsy man-upstairs view of God that is inappropriately over-familiar. Picturing God as holy renders him the respect to which he is entitled. It also admits some healthy things about our own need for humility.

But if we are not careful, it also leads us down some blind alleys. We may begin to think that God is unapproachable. After all, he told Moses: "You cannot see my face, for no one may see me and live" (Exodus 33:20). All through the Old Testament, catching a glimpse of the Almighty meant signing your death warrant.

Many people think that God is so holy that you and I can't get anywhere near him. The more we are aware of our sinfulness, the greater the distance becomes! The more we need God, the harder he is to find! "Who may ascend the hill of the LORD? Who may stand in his holy place? He who has clean hands and a pure heart, who does not lift up his soul to an idol or swear by what is false" (Psalm 24:3-4). That cuts me out of the line! Who among us qualifies to climb the sacred mountain? None. Not even the falsely self-righteous. We are all sinners, every one of us. And the beautiful, necessary, and correct idea of the holiness of God becomes a barrier. Any way of access is blocked by the vast differences between God and each one of us.

It is unfair to think the Old Testament teaches that God turns up his nose or gives us the cold shoulder. On the contrary, it paints a vivid picture of a God who is unusually involved in the lives of individuals and the history of nations. God is busily at work, doing what he wants to do on earth. With a great goal in mind, he spares some and sacrifices others. He temporarily rescinds the laws of nature when it serves his purposes. He overrules human authority and politics. Moreover, he develops deep bonds with certain individuals. There is an affinity of the Divine Spirit with the human spirit—in the psalmist's words, "Deep calls to deep" (Psalm 42:7). A mere human being can claim, "The LORD is my shepherd" (Psalm 23:1).

One of the most profound statements describing the tension between God's remoteness and his nearness is found in Isaiah: "This is what the high and lofty One says—he who lives forever, whose name is holy: 'I live in a high and holy place, but also with him who is contrite and lowly in spirit, to revive the spirit of the lowly and to revive the heart of the contrite'" (Isaiah 57:15).

The Truth

Jesus Christ taught that *God is actually looking for us!* He is not only a shepherd, but the Good Shepherd who seeks a lost sheep. Our Father-who-is-in-heaven doesn't sit in an office waiting for us to make an appointment so we can tell him how badly we have misbehaved. Instead, he cares so much that he comes searching for us. When he finds us he encourages us to come home with him. He desires to be our friend. He is restless until we are home with him.

If you are not a Christian, take a good look at that paragraph again. Do you want to know what is distinctive about Christianity? Have you been curious to know how it is different from all the other religions of the world? Do you want to know how Christ can help you live with yourself? There is your answer—God is your friend.

Want to see it in action? Look at Jesus Christ. Jesus said, "Anyone who has seen me has seen the Father" (John 14:9). What disturbed all those self-righteous Pharisees was Jesus' friendliness with "sinners." He buddied up with all the wrong people. He accepted dinner invitations that any self-respecting person would quickly decline. He was seen laughing and talking with "bad" people. The "good" people were offended.

Not only did Jesus say and show that God loves the worst people in the world, but he also assured us that this love is personal. His friendship is on a one-to-one basis. Jesus is emphatic about this. He says that the very hairs of our heads are known and numbered by God, that God even notices the ups and downs of individual sparrows!

We wonder how this can be. Perhaps you have tried to telephone the top executive of a giant corporation. You can speak with a dozen secretaries and two dozen vice-presidents. Each will ask you—while the long distance charges are running up—how to spell your name. The President of the United States has a telephone, but try giving him a call!

God is not some kind of amplified super-president. When I was younger, I always wondered how God could possibly hear and answer all of the prayers emanating from the world's churches on Sunday. I visualized a harried switchboard operator, plugging in a tangled rat's nest of patch cords.

Only recently did I gain an insight that clearly showed me how wrong this mental image of God and prayer was. My son brought home a print-out from his high-school computer class. All of the public schools had terminals linked to a huge computer downtown. This great machine scanned all of the many terminals on a rotating basis in a split second. If there was some work demanding its attention, it paused long enough to hear the request, figure the answer, print the results, and then started scanning again. David had worked on that machine for nearly an hour, but at the end it recorded the amount of time spent on his problems as only 3.6 seconds!

A computer is a finite machine. God is infinite Spirit, bathing all creation with his living presence, not limited by time or space. With a clear understanding of this, Jesus gave us his calm assurance that God cares for us *individually.*

It will make all the difference in the world for you if you can share that understanding. God is neither out to get you nor hiding from you. He loves you. He is looking for you. He wants to help. He cares. He wants to be your friend.

Your prayer life will lose its emptiness and gain a vitality you never imagined possible once you have gotten over this hurdle. Great spiritual leaders through the centuries have agreed that genuine prayer is far more than words or thoughts directed to God. It is friendship with God. St. Teresa of Avila said prayer is "developing friendship with the person who we know loves us."[9]

When you arrive at the place in your life where this idea becomes fact for you, you will be ready to comprehend how a holy God can also be a forgiving God.

> But because of his great love for us, God, who is rich in mercy, made us alive with Christ even when we were dead in transgressions—it is by grace you have been saved.
> *Ephesians 2:4-5*

Let It Hit Home

❏ What was your earliest concept of God?

❏ How has that concept changed throughout your life? What caused it to change?

4

The Forgiving Nature of God

God forgives—forgives not capriciously, but with wise, definite, Divine pre-arrangement; forgives universally, on the grounds of an atonement and on the condition of repentance and faith.
Richard Salter Storrs

If there is one thing you can absolutely depend upon, it is the forgiveness of God. I say that with the full weight of Scripture as my authority. There is no way we can read and believe the Bible and have any doubt about this. The One who fashioned us of earthly elements wants to forgive our earthly sins.

The more you read the Bible, the less you will want to challenge the paragraph above. It would be an overwhelming task to review even a portion of the biblical support for what I have asserted so boldly. Still, the idea may be new to you. If your only conceptions of God are based on your childhood fears and scowling, pulpit-pounding preachers, you need to listen to at least a few representative passages from the Bible itself. Let God speak for himself rather than through an interpreter. I believe God's Spirit will make the meaning clear for anyone who will read the

Bible prayerfully. Moreover, none of the verses I am going to call to your attention now are controversial. There is nothing difficult or obscure in them. What they say about the forgiving nature of God is clear and straightforward.

Old Testament Examples

Sometimes I hear it said that the God of the Old Testament is a God of anger and wrath, and that it took Jesus and the New Testament to introduce a warmer and more forgiving side to God's nature. Nonsense! Nothing could be more incorrect. The God who is busy in the pages of the New Testament is the same God who is at work in the Old Testament. Instead of changing God's attitude, Christ became the fullest expression of it. Yes, there are moments in the Old Testament when God is reported to be exasperated by human behavior. Who could blame him? But behind that divine displeasure is a constant, caring, loving, and forgiving nature. So let's start with the Old Testament.

Here is a summary of it all in Nehemiah 9:16-17:

> But they, our forefathers, became arrogant and stiff-necked, and did not obey your commands. They refused to listen and failed to remember the miracles you performed among them. They became stiff-necked and in their rebellion appointed a leader in order to return to their slavery. But you are a forgiving God, gracious and compassionate, slow to anger and abounding in love. Therefore you did not desert them . . .

If you read the remainder of that chapter of Nehemiah, you will see how wonderfully patient God is even when we blatantly provoke him.

The Psalms are a treasury of comfort for us on this subject. I will single out only three brief references to demonstrate what I mean.

> You forgave the iniquity of your people
> and covered all their sins. *Psalm 85:2*
>
> You are forgiving and good, O Lord,
> abounding in love to all who call to you. *Psalm 86:5*
>
> If you, O LORD, kept a record of sins,
> O Lord, who could stand?
> But with you there is forgiveness;
> therefore you are feared. *Psalm 130:3-4*

And what about the prophets? Aren't they full of fire and condemnation? Don't they shake a finger in our faces and tell us we are all going to hell because we are so bad? Listen as they speak.

> "Come now, let us reason together,"
> says the LORD.
> "Though your sins are like scarlet,
> they shall be as white as snow;
> though they are red as crimson,
> they shall be like wool. *Isaiah 1:18*

I have swept away your offenses like a cloud,
your sins like the morning mist.
Return to me,
for I have redeemed you. *Isaiah 44:22*

Seek the LORD while he may be found;
call on him while he is near.
Let the wicked forsake his way
and the evil man his thoughts.
Let him turn to the LORD, and he will have mercy
    on him,
and to our God, for he will freely pardon. *Isaiah 55:6-7*

"No longer will a man teach his neighbor,
or a man his brother, saying, 'Know the LORD,'
because they will all know me,
from the least of them to the greatest," declares
    the LORD.
"For I will forgive their wickedness
and will remember their sins no more." *Jeremiah 31:34*

I will cleanse them from all the sin they have
    committed against me and will forgive all their
    sins of rebellion against me. *Jeremiah 33:8*

There is no other god like you, O LORD; you forgive
    the sins of your people . . . *Micah 7:18, GNB*

Do you need more to be convinced? I have only scratched the surface. Read the short book of Hosea.

See how God's annoyance at our disgusting behavior is replaced at the end with undiminished love:

> I will heal their waywardncss
> and love them freely,
> for my anger has turned away from them. *Hosea 14:4*

New Testament Examples

The witness of the Old Testament is clear—God loves us deeply and wants to forgive us. But we are not limited to that ancient witness. The New Testament continues and fulfills the story of God's love. Jesus asked, "Don't you believe that I am in the Father, and that the Father is in me? The words I say to you are not just my own. Rather, it is the Father, living in me, who is doing his work. Believe me when I say that I am in the Father and the Father is in me; or at least believe on the evidence of the miracles themselves" (John 14:10).

What do we see when we look at Jesus? We see a person who forgives without hesitation, someone who even disregards his own safety and accepts severe criticism in order to assure another of God's forgiveness. Read Luke 5:17-26 and John 8:1-11 for examples of his selfless forgiving.

Read Christ's parable known as "The Prodigal Son." As the young man returns from his rebellious independence, he has a little speech all memorized: "I will set out and go back to my father and say to him: Father, I have sinned against heaven and against you.

I am no longer worthy to be called your son; make me like one of your hired men" (Luke 15:18-19).

Notice the way Christ tells it. When the son starts his piece, the father interrupts him with an embrace of love. He never gets to finish offering his deal: "I'll work for you like a servant if you take me back." The loving father won't listen to it! Instead he calls for his best robe, a ring, shoes, and announces a feast of celebration and joy.

Watching Christ at work among us is an impressive demonstration of the unconditional love God has for us. Even when the rich young ruler refused to accept Christ's offer, the gospel tells us that "Jesus looked at him and loved him" (Mark 10:21). He told his followers that they must forgive others "seventy times seven" (Matthew 18:22), or without limit.

Forgiveness of sin is at the very heart of the New Testament. Christ, even as he was dying upon the cross, said, "Father, forgive them, for they do not know what they are doing" (Luke 23:34).

Dangers of Shallow Understanding

The sketchy outline above should be enough to convince us. Without a doubt, the Bible teaches us to depend upon the forgiving nature of God. Unfortunately, this opens the way to some erroneous conclusions.

If we accept God's forgiveness as fact, we may begin to believe that the things we do, say, and think are unimportant to the Almighty. If God will ultimately forgive me, then what difference does it make what I do? Stewart's Law of Retroaction states: "It is easier to get forgiveness than permission."[10]

This is the very can of worms Paul opened when he wrote and preached so enthusiastically about salvation by grace. God's love for us is a free gift. It does not depend upon how good we are because we are all sinners, even the do-gooders. We cannot earn God's affection by our deeds, our behavior, or our works. Paul rejoiced in his discovery that we don't have to. Our forgiveness is unmerited. "God demonstrates his own love for us in this: While we were still sinners, Christ died for us" (Romans 5:8).

For a culture saturated with a legalistic understanding of religious life, this was a tremendous breakthrough. People were beginning to understand what Jesus was saying. Sadly, many new Christians thought it gave them a license to sin. If they could disregard rules and still have God's love and forgiveness, then why bother at all?

People have always been that way. We still are. In communities where people know there is no follow-up on parking tickets, some never pay the fine. Others have a stack of unheeded citations. Before our government became stricter, many scholarship loans were never paid back. If we can get by with it, we generally try to. Certainly there are many people who live on a higher moral plane, who do what is honest and right even when there are no penalties. May their tribe increase! Nevertheless, if you are running a business, you must be realistic and take into account the human tendency to get away with whatever we can.

God's method of dealing with us is so different. The apostle Paul tells us that God will wipe out our debt—

we don't have to pay him back. No wonder people misunderstood him.

Paul settled the issue with clarity. "What shall we say, then? Shall we go on sinning so that grace may increase? By no means! We died to sin; how can we live in it any longer?" (Romans 6:1-2) Instead of living decently in order to make God love us, we do so *because* God loves us. Our behavior is a response to his generous love, not the ticket that buys it.

Sometimes when we are finally convinced of the forgiving nature of God, we mistakenly conclude that it must be an easy thing for God to forgive us. Like a millionaire who has no difficulty paying an indigent's electric bill, we assume God forgives us with little or no cost to himself. This has been called "cheap grace." The Bible is so grand in its assurances of pardon that some may think God forgives us with a wave of his hand. A trifling matter, human sin.

The very opposite is true. The Bible insists that sin costs us, our families, our neighborhoods, the world. Our sins will send bills to unborn generations, even as we are paying for those from previous decades. Human sin is expensive. It exacts payment in dollars, tears, and blood. And make no mistake about it, the debt accrued by our sin is far greater than our ability to pay. Even our greatest losses of happiness, reputation, and position will not offset it.

The one who pays is God. I have been sharing with you in a straightforward manner for four chapters, and I'm not going to plunge into syrupy theology now. But if you have an imagination, use it. It will prevent you from taking your forgiveness lightly. And afterwards, it will help you to forgive yourself.

Imagine, if you can, what it is like to be God. That's a tall order, I know. Jesus said God is like a good Father who loves his children. If you are a parent, you will need no further guidance. If you are not, try to imagine what it must be like to love a child dearly. You have nurtured it from the cradle, watched it grow and develop, enjoyed every new stage along the way. You have invested a lot of time and emotion. You have awakened at night to the hacking cough of an immature bronchial tract and rushed to a hospital's emergency room for repair of some injury. You have bought toys, read books aloud, laughed together at cartoons on TV. You have wiped away tears from a bully-blackened eye and gone out of your way to provide for education. You have seen shoes outgrown long before they are worn out and you have sacrificed to buy designer jeans. You have answered a hundred questions and evaded two hundred. In many ways, yours has been a thankless task, but the one uncontrollable, overriding, inescapable fact is your love for this child. You would wrestle a bear or fight city hall to protect him or her.

Now multiply that by infinity. Imagine our Creator caring for all his creatures like that. Think how you would react if the police telephoned to say they had your son in jail on a drug charge. Consider your grief when your sixteen-year-old daughter runs off with a thrice-divorced man of thirty-six. Stand on the bloody pavement where your son's motorcycle has collided with a truck and feel the constriction in your guts we call a breaking heart. Remind yourself that you feel these things for one reason only—the attachment of love. You'll discover that love costs you; it makes you vulnerable to exceeding pain. Do you think it hurts like that to be God?

And you are not through yet. Now you've got to go bail that boy out of jail. You have to open your door and let your disillusioned, desperate daughter back into your home. You need to be standing there by the hospital bed when your little stunt man regains consciousness. In each case your child will want to know if you still love him. Terrified, remorseful eyes will search for assurance. Will it be easy to give?

The cheap thing would be to let the kid rot in jail, to kick your daughter out of the house and trouble yourself no further. By a wave of your hand you could deny all responsibility and tell the hell-driver you hope he has finally learned a few lessons.

What will cost you the most is what your troubled child needs the most—loving forgiveness.

It is no different with God. Isaiah's poetry about the Suffering Servant gives us some insight:

Surely he took up our infirmities
and carried our sorrows,
yet we considered him stricken by God,
smitten by him, and afflicted.
But he was pierced for our transgressions,
he was crushed for our iniquities;
the punishment that brought us peace was upon
    him,
and by his wounds we are healed.
We all, like sheep, have gone astray,
each of us has turned to his own way;
And the LORD has laid on him
the iniquity of us all. *Isaiah 53:4-6*

Christians have identified the servant in that prophecy, and others like it, as Jesus Christ. Add to it the fullest understanding you can wring from John 3:16—"For God so loved the world that he gave his only begotten Son . . ." (KJV). Perhaps now you are beginning to see. Loving forgiveness is the most expensive thing there is. Love may be a spendthrift, but the payment will always come due. And the lover will pay. Grace is free only to the one who receives it. Forgiving us costs God plenty.

Why are you reading this book? How have you helped to crucify God's Son? What did you do? Steal something? Hurt somebody? Split a church? Have an affair? Let down a team? Destroy someone's reputation? Whatever it is, however terrible the combination and consequences, you can absolutely count on this: God wants to forgive you. At great cost to himself, he wants to cancel your debt.

Now who are you not to forgive yourself? Are your standards higher than his? And yet I know your problem. It's not what you think that matters, it's how you feel. You may agree with everything I've said and still feel "down." Let's talk this over in the next chapter.

I tell you that . . . there will be more rejoicing in heaven over one sinner who repents than over ninety-nine righteous persons who do not need to repent.
Luke 15:7

Let It Hit Home

❑ What has helped you most in seeing God as a friend who seeks reconciliation?

❑ If you cannot see God in this way, what do you think the reason is?

PART THREE

Roadblocks to Guilt-Free Living

5

The Problem Is How You Feel

(Not What You Think)

*Conscience is merely our own judgment of
the right or wrong of our actions, and so can
never be a safe guide unless enlightened
by the word of God.*
Tryon Edwards

We have two ways of "thinking"—with our heads and with our hearts. The more difficult the issue or stressful the circumstances, the more likely the heart will overrule the head. It is one thing to intellectually believe God is forgiving. It is entirely different to *feel* you have received his forgiveness.

Earlier we stated that confession was the first step toward forgiving yourself. But it is only the first step. Others must follow.

The child says to his mother, "I told a lie."

"It's all right," replies the supportive parent. "I forgive you."

"Yes, but I still told a lie."

Confession may have brought with it a tremendous emotional release. You may have wept or laughed uncontrollably. For the moment you may have had a better appetite or enjoyed more restful sleep. But gradually, the old feelings begin to creep back. The memory is still there. You have had no convincing assurance of anyone, let alone God, actually forgiving you. If you stop here, you will go right on saying, "I know God forgives me, but I can't forgive myself." The quotations from the Bible may have battered your mind into acceptance, but your heart still needs convincing. Self-forgiveness can be more complex than a religious realization. We can know we are forgiven without feeling forgiven.

I remind you again that you may need to seek some competent face-to-face help with your difficulties at this level. The printed page can only go so far. There may be additional questions you need to wrestle with. There may be doors you have kept locked inside yourself for so long you can't remember where they are or how to find the keyhole. A patient, sympathetic counselor will help you explore emotional territory you may otherwise overlook.

Here are a few examples of how your ordinary human nature can prevent you from feeling forgiven.

Damaged Self-Esteem

Whenever you miss your mark, disappoint yourself, lose control, and say or do something vicious or ridiculous, you chip away a piece of your self-worth. You begin to look down on yourself. In subtle ways you may neither notice nor understand, you will begin punishing yourself.

Have you seen pictures of the self-flagellation in Philippine or Iranian streets during holy festivals? Barebacked young men walk in solemn procession rhythmically throwing cat-o'-nine-tails over their shoulders, raising welts and drawing blood. You may think this is horribly primitive, pointless, and disgusting. And yet, if you have acknowledged your sin, are convinced that the Bible assures you of God's forgiveness, and still can't forgive yourself, you are probably busy whipping yourself. Perhaps you overeat or get drunk. Maybe you don't turn in a good day's work or you refuse to accept a compliment, pay no attention to personal grooming, or don't get enough exercise. On the other hand, you may force yourself to jog an extra mile.

It is easier to persecute yourself than to accept God's forgiveness when your self-esteem has been damaged. But there is a way out. Remind yourself that God loves you—you are his child. Yes, you have grieved your heavenly Father, but he still loves you. Jesus said, "Whoever comes to me I will never drive away" (John 6:37).

God not only loves and accepts you, he can help you to be important to someone else. This is the surest repair for damaged self-esteem. You will never feel any value in yourself until you are valuable to another person. A feeling of worthlessness is the result of meaningless relationships. God gave you life for a purpose. You are needed. You have a unique responsibility that no one else can fulfill. When you begin to live purposefully with others you will naturally find it easier to live with yourself.

You will be amazed by how quickly God will answer a prayer to be given someone to care for. Your neighborhood is full of people who need you. Go to a nursing home and walk down the corridor. Perfect strangers will reach out to you, desperate for your attention. If you let them, they will hold your hand and talk for hours. There is no excuse for you to feel as though you are not needed.

All the dictators and despots in this world are suffering from unredeemed self-esteem. This applies to everyone from that irritating person where you work to the clowns who have made the news by waving swords and pistols in our faces. Consider people like Noriega and Hussein. They created a tremor in the world. But they were insecure personalities who tried to compensate by becoming "powerful." They were looking for a little self-respect. Dissatisfied with themselves as persons, they tried to achieve it by controlling and manipulating others.

Jesus was tempted to be an earthly achiever. He could have risen to great political and military power. He had the kind of charisma that would have made that possible. What so many of us miss is that Christ did not need to do that. He had an extraordinarily healthy personality and understood that worldly authority and prestige are passing and worthless things. He did not suffer from a low self-esteem that needed bolstering by dominating the public. Nothing in him would be fed by exploiting others.

When the rulers of this world make their subjects feel a lack of dignity while they themselves are maneuvering for power and authority, they are actually doing nothing at all to help themselves out of their own low self-esteem. The only way any of us will ever improve our feelings about ourselves is to begin to improve our feelings about others. Increase your neighbor's self-esteem and you will increase your own. It's that simple. That is the great value in being a servant as Christ commands. The way to accept yourself is to accept others. The way to love yourself is to love others. That's the way God made it. That's the way God wants it. That's the only way out.

Resentment

Here is a stinker! Resentment is a natural human response, but it is always damaging. In the next section we will examine in greater detail how forgiving yourself directly involves other people. For now, recall how Jesus taught us to pray, "Forgive us our debts, as we also have forgiven our debtors" (Matthew 6:12).

Resentment is a barrier to God's forgiveness. Until we have forgiven the person, the institution, the system, or the circumstances attendant upon our fall, we will never feel forgiven.

Again, there is help. Remember the other person is also God's child. Try to be understanding and patient. It is a natural thing that you should sometimes resent the things said or done to you, even if they come from your loved ones. The people you care about are precisely the ones most likely to annoy you. You don't resent the actions of faceless drivers on the Interstate. You can be upset by them, but you are indifferent toward them as persons. Living in close proximity with family is guaranteed to produce some friction once in a while. The great saints would tell you it is a tremendous spiritual discipline to take a few lumps and swallow your pride.

Resentment is directly related to guilt. Both spring from anger. "Guilt is anger directed at ourselves—at what we did or did not do. Resentment is anger directed at others—at what they did or did not do."[11] Remind yourself that resentment is always a negative influence. Don't allow yourself to become obsessed with mental revenge. I make you this promise: *The more forgiving you are of others, the more you will feel forgiven yourself. The more you give away, the more you will receive.*

It all comes down to showing a little mercy. In the Beatitudes Jesus says, "Blessed are the merciful: for they shall obtain mercy" (Matthew 5:7, KJV). The thought could be expressed this way: "Blessed are those who do not collect resentments."

Do you think you can't control your feelings? You are wrong. Your feelings can be educated by control or they can be allowed to run wild. It is possible to master your imagination. Mercy, the opposite of resentment, begins in your thoughts. You can cultivate a kindly attitude as easily as you can nurse your grievances. I have known people who could keep up a feud for years. They wait patiently for the moment when they can pay someone back. Feeling and action act and react upon each other. Indulge your feelings and they get stronger.

If you refuse to express love, acceptance, and forgiveness to others, you are standing in your own way. You are preventing yourself from sharing in forgiveness. This is not an idealistic religious precept. It is the way it is. There is no freedom like the release that comes when you drop resentments.

Religious Legalism

Sadly, a distorted experience of "religion" can also be a hindrance. If you have been nurtured by narrow, legalistic religious teaching, you will have an extremely difficult time believing in your heart what your brain knows is true. You may think of God as a kind of vending machine. Put a couple of quarters in and something comes out—most of the time. Put nothing in and you get nothing out. If you get a freebie, something must be broken.

Polite people say we should not criticize religion. But Christ never took that advice. In fact, Jesus was a devastating critic of the religiosity in his day. Few things annoyed him more than to see religious professionals interfering with the flow of God's love. Do you think it's wrong to be critical of religion? Jesus said, "Woe to you, teachers of the law and Pharisees, you hypocrites! You shut the kingdom of heaven in men's faces. You yourselves do not enter, nor will you let those enter who are trying to. Woe to you, teachers of the law and Pharisees, you hypocrites! You travel over land and sea to win a single convert, and when he becomes one, you make him twice as much a son of hell as you are" (Matthew 23:13-15).

Our Lord spoke in these sharp terms at some length. Some New Testament scholars have suggested that early Christians twisted his comments and made them stronger than when he originally spoke them. Whether or not that may be, it remains clear that Jesus has strong feelings about this. One of the things that infuriated his enemies most was his criticism of religious teaching. "You blind guides! You strain out a gnat but swallow a camel. . . . Woe to you, teachers of the law and Pharisees, you hypocrites! You are like whitewashed tombs, which look beautiful on the outside but on the inside are full of dead men's bones and everything unclean. In the same way, on the outside you appear to people as righteous but on the inside you are full of hypocrisy and wickedness" (Matthew 23:24, 27-28).

Francis de Sales, very much in tune with the spirit of Christ, expressed the problem beautifully. "People naturally think their way is best. The person who fasts thinks this makes him very devout, even though he may harbor hatred in his heart. Another is a total abstainer from drink who tricks and cheats his neighbor, drinking, as it were, his neighbor's blood. Another is sure he is devout because he says many prayers, and yet his language is arrogant and abrasive at home and at work. Another gives liberally to the poor, but is unable to forgive his enemies. Another forgives his enemies but doesn't pay his bills. All of these could be thought of as devout, but they are not. They only hint at devotion."[12]

Some clergymen generate their income by inducing guilt. They may mean well, but they malign Jesus Christ and butcher the sacred Scriptures. Many of them represent the umpteenth generation of Pharisees, passing on the poison of preachers long dead. The pietistic religion they proclaim seems easy enough, but it is toxic. If you have received a nearly lethal dose of this substandard Christianity, you will have difficulty forgiving yourself.

But there is a way out. Seek the spiritual maturity you have been denied. Ask yourself some stinging questions about what you have been told and evaluate the personalities of those who have communicated the faith to you. Compare what you have heard with what you can read for yourself in the Bible. Replace immature fear with adult trust. Don't imagine that you can do anything (or refrain from doing anything) that will make one particle of difference in removing the guilt you carry. Jesus died for your sins; you don't have to. Sing the familiar hymn:

Not the labors of my hands
Can fulfill Thy law's demands . . .
Nothing in my hand I bring,
Simply to Thy cross I cling;
Naked, come to Thee for dress,
Helpless, look to Thee for grace . . .[13]

Some of the guilt we feel is not the result of our own choices. It was handed to us by others. We'll try to understand this problem next.

Godly sorrow brings repentance that leads to salvation and leaves no regret, but worldly sorrow brings death.
2 Corinthians 7:10

Let It Hit Home

☐ What is your greatest barrier to accepting forgiveness?

☐ Think through the events of the past day or week. How many of your reactions can be traced to the way you felt at the time, as opposed to what you thought about the situation?

6

Inherited Guilt

The mind of guilt is full of scorpions.
Shakespeare

We are born into families. We do not hatch from eggs buried in the sand. Everyone with a navel has a mother. It is now clear that the months we spend cozily in the womb are not a time of isolation. As a fetus we hear and respond to sounds, conversations, and stimuli of all kinds. Because our first blood is our mother's blood, we eat what she eats, drink what she drinks. If she takes drugs, we take drugs. If she is exposed to x-rays, we are exposed to x-rays. We have no choice in the matter. For our lengthy period of gestation we are one with our mothers. We begin to experience life long before we are "born," and our experience is our mother's experience.

People are different. Mothers vary. When Mother's Day rolls around each spring, how do you feel about it? Perhaps it is difficult for you to resonate with the syrupy sweetness of greeting cards. You may have been blessed with an angel, or you may have coped with someone far down the ladder from sainthood. Mothers come in all varieties.

The same is true for Dad. Many people have a difficult time with the Lord's Prayer simply because it begins, "Our Father." For them, *father* is either an absent figure or an oppressive one.

One thing needs to be recognized about parents. They are amateurs. They conceive children without any idea of what to do with them. They have no experience when the first baby arrives, and because children are as different as parents, they don't know much more when subsequent ones are born. They may attend all kinds of classes on "parenting" and still be helplessly ignorant when really tough situations arise. Even professional counselors, who can guide others out of tangled messes, are often tongue-tied and without insight when it comes to their own children. Life is complicated and stressful today. Even intimate communities have competing cultures. The very best parents frequently fail to give us what we need. Mistakes happen. Personalities, as well as bodies, are wounded.

What is the model of a healthy, functioning, nurturing family? You won't find one on TV. The contemporary families you see on the screen are fictions from the minds of writers who may have no genuine family experience of their own. They write about situations calculated to be marketable. If you watch an old rerun of the families from the fifties or sixties you are still watching idealized fiction with little contact with reality. Someone said those early scripts present "happy problems with happy solutions," and that's never been the way most of life is lived. There may not be a perfect example of a perfect family.

The fact remains—all of us were cared for as infants. If we survived someone took care of us. A lot of work goes into getting a human child to the point of independence. The movie, "Home Alone," was enormously popular, but it clearly told an impossible, daydreaming story. None of the stunts this eight-year-old Rambo pulled would work out in the real world. For years we remain physically and emotionally dependent upon someone older.

Of course there are thousands of latchkey children today. Most American school districts are reporting that more than half of their pupils are coming from single-parent homes. Many kids are streetwise at tender ages. They have to be or they don't survive. A first grader once said to me, "When you go to the restroom you have to look under the partition. If you see any feet, they will jump on you."

All of which is to say that we are exposed to huge influences while growing up. Good things happen, and also disturbing things. We have been shaped and molded, groomed and polished, scoured and scuffed by other hands. It is impossible to simply walk away from home, however good or bad it may have been. We carry emotional baggage. We may leave home, but home does not leave us. Consciously or unconsciously, we remember what has happened. We may have "grown up," but we are still children inside. The events that caused our feelings are gone, but the feelings themselves are still with us. We may think, "Nothing is wrong, don't worry," but our feelings override our minds. We may look adult, even geriatric, but continue to use the little gambits and games that got us through a tough childhood. These childish responses were ways of coping. They may have helped us survive *then*, but they cause conflict and stress *now*. We dislike this automatic behavior in ourselves. But we have a hard time discovering how we acquired it, and an even harder time changing it. Let's face some facts together.

Dysfunctional Families and Their Legacy

It is difficult to present a model of a perfect family because there are no perfect families. Even the best make mistakes. I grew up surrounded by love in a caring atmosphere, but I still have childhood memories that are very painful. Some of them stand out like flashes in early years when I was much too young to store away continuous blocks of memory. For instance, I can vividly recall being yelled at by my mother. I wanted a bowl of cornflakes. She was busy, so I sat down on the kitchen floor with a bowl and poured some milk into it. The cereal would come next. When she spotted what her two-year-old was doing she let out a terrible howl and told me to stop. She grabbed the milk bottle from me and slammed the refrigerator door. She must have been struggling with some kitchen agitation at the time, or perhaps she was trying to figure out what to do about her elderly father who had been causing some problems for her. I don't know. She does not recall the incident and can offer no light on her state of mind at the time. All I know is that I felt horribly misunderstood and ashamed. I recently stood in that newly remodeled kitchen and recalled the very spot where it happened so long ago. Fortunately, I could also remember that spring the second or third year of my life when the back door was open, and the songs of wrens drifted into the kitchen on warm breezes. I never doubted that my mother loved me. When we are secure, we can tolerate such moments without being damaged.

Others have much more disturbing memories. Christine Herbruck, in *Breaking the Cycle of Child Abuse,* reports the following incident from the life of one of her subjects: "I was making Christmas cookies with my mother . . . Since I was almost five at the time, I was allowed to help her stir and measure for the first time. I can remember how the kitchen smelled, kind of wet and warm and sweet. I felt really good . . . My mother told me to go and measure out a pint of something. I don't even remember what it was, but I do remember the feeling in the pit of my stomach. I got this horrible feeling. I had no idea what a pint was. I kind of stood there for a minute—it was a very long minute. I knew I was going to ruin everything, that this was the end of our good time. Finally I told her I didn't know which one the pint was. I'll never forget having to say that. She was standing right there in front of me with the rolling pin in one hand, and she picked up the cookie sheet in the other. I just stood there. She hit me first with the one and then the other and then with both of them at the same time. She yelled and screamed at me—how stupid I was—how no good I was—how dumb I was—how bad and useless I was—how ugly and stupid I was. I just stood there. I was right. I had ruined it."[14]

The woman who related this incident said that she still gets that same sick feeling whenever she doesn't know something, as though her mother were standing there with her rolling pin and cookie sheet.

Much is said today of dysfunctional families. A dysfunctional family is one that causes damage to its members by the things that happen or don't happen within the family itself. Sometimes it is outright abuse. Sometimes it is a denial of what would ordinarily be expected as right and proper. It only takes one family member to create an atmosphere where the entire family suffers.

The destabilizing influence is often alcohol. But it can just as readily be drug abuse, fighting parents, divorce, neglect, sexual abuse, verbal assault, or actual physical injury. Perhaps a parent is mentally ill or extremely rigid about religious matters. Whenever parents find ways to terrorize, ignore, reject, isolate, or corrupt their children, a dysfunctional family exists.

Usually the problem is not faced within the family. It is not that it is denied. It is simply ignored. Members of families with a problem alcoholic do not openly discuss alcoholism. Mom's drinking becomes a "family secret." This unspoken agreement to keep the secret is more destructive than anyone can imagine. It's like failing to tell the doctor your side hurts. Until you admit the problem you will avoid treatment. Families tend to treat as taboo the very thing that is most damaging to its members.

One of the grim facts of life is that we become what we live with, and we pass it on to our children. Dysfunctional families produce more dysfunctional families. We do what we have learned. If your father cursed you, you will probably curse your children. This is a vicious spiral. The individual who emerges from such a situation has a lot more ahead than simply marrying and rearing a family. It is a matter of escaping a trap, of breaking a cycle. The clinical odds are that seven out of ten who were abused as children will abuse their own. Often the daughter of an alcoholic will marry an alcoholic.

Guidance from the Scriptures

The Old Testament expresses the phenomenon this way: "The Lord is slow to anger, abounding in love and forgiving sin and rebellion. Yet he does not leave the guilty unpunished; he punishes the children for the sin of the fathers to the third and fourth generation" (Numbers 14:18). This inherited guilt doesn't mean that God holds us responsible for the sins of our parents. As we will see in a moment, we are responsible for our own sins, not Mom's and Dad's. This statement about the third and fourth generations paying the price for parental blunders is first stated in the Ten Commandments and then quoted in many other places in the Old Testament. In essence, it is saying the same thing we have been thinking about together. Hurting families produce hurting families.

The Bible insists that children need parental guidance. Without it we get into all kinds of additional mischief. "The rod of correction imparts wisdom, but a child left to itself disgraces his mother" (Proverbs 29:15). In the book of Ezekiel we catch a glimpse of popular gossip in the ancient world. "Everyone who quotes proverbs will quote this proverb about you: 'Like mother, like daughter.' You are a true daughter of your mother, who despised her husband and her children; and you are a true sister of your sisters, who despised their husbands and their children . . ." (Ezekiel 16:44-45).

In a more positive approach on the influence of families, the prophet Jeremiah speaks for God.

> I will give them singleness of heart and action, so that they will always fear me for their own good and the good of their children after them. *Jeremiah 32:39*

The most famous verse of them all in this vein can be found in Proverbs.

> Train a child in the way he should go, and when he is old he will not turn from it. *Proverbs 22:6*

But here is the important lesson for application to our need right now. The Scriptures assure us that our home's influence is strong in both positive and negative ways, but it is not inescapable. We still have freedom of choice and remain responsible for ourselves and our own behavior. The Bible will not allow us to pin the blame for our actions on the family we grew up with. "In those days people will no longer say, 'The fathers have eaten sour grapes, and the children's teeth are set on edge.' Instead, everyone will die for his own sin; whoever eats sour grapes—his own teeth will be set on edge" (Jeremiah 31:29-30).

Some of us can come through a rough beginning and still turn out to be creative, productive, model citizens. The rest of us can take courage from the teaching of Scripture. No matter how broken you may be, you can be fixed with God's help. The heart of the Christian message is that we can be born again. Christ can change us. We do not have to remain as we are.

It is in this spirit that the New Testament advises us,

> Fathers, do not exasperate your children; instead, bring them up in the training and instruction of the Lord. *Ephesians 6:4*

Jesus said, "Be merciful, just as your Father is merciful" (Luke 6:36).

Recognizing a Problem

We naturally accept things as they are given to us when we are children. Unless we are exposed to different places and different ways of doing things we never guess that life could be any other way.

I grew up in the humid marshes of the mid-Atlantic region of the United Sates. I thought stifling summer heat and mosquitoes were "normal." One August when I was about twelve years old I was a guest for a week at a cottage high in the mountains of North Carolina. I will never forget the sensation of breathing in deep gulps of cool, dry mountain air. There was something heady about it. I wondered why anyone would live in Tidewater when they could live in the mountains and breath air like that.

We consider normal whatever context we are born into. If Mom brings a new man home every night, that is normal. If Dad gets drunk every weekend, that is normal. If I have to fix breakfast for my little sister because we are alone, that is normal. If my parents fight, that is normal. When these are the only things we know, they don't seem as peculiar as they would to one who knows another way. One of our children's friends was astonished after a visit to our home: "Your parents don't yell at each other!"

It might take a crisis of some kind to bring conditions into focus. A marriage can fall apart, someone might get sick, or there could be a serious accident. Suddenly insight will dawn. "Things are not right. They have never been right. This is not the way to live. We are in trouble."

Maybe that crisis never occurred for you. As you read you are wondering whether or not you may be the product of a dysfunctional family, or just a kid with nice parents who sometimes lost control of themselves. You can find the answer by understanding the typical qualities of a dysfunctional family.

Normal families enjoy being together. They respect each other. They like to tell stories and laugh a lot. They honestly care what happens to all the other members of the family. The dysfunctional family is held together by rules. Each member knows what is expected. Rigidity is supreme. "Of course you will go to Grandma's for Christmas. We always go to Grandma's for Christmas." There is no room for alternatives. Not even for desirable alternatives. You can do the right thing or you can do the wrong thing. There is no flexibility.

A serious problem with the rules in a dysfunctional family is that they are forever changing. Life is chaotic and unpredictable. What may bring you praise one day brings criticism the next. Children are stunned when what they think is the correct behavior suddenly gets them into trouble. They are confused when doing the right thing doesn't spare them the misery they wanted to avoid. "If I don't play my records, Mom won't have one of her spells." But Mom has her spell anyway. "If I am a good boy, Dad won't drink this weekend and throw things through the walls." But Dad does drink, and his violence is terrifying. The child tries to do what is pleasing but usually gives up in discouragement.

Addictions of all kinds are commonplace in dysfunctional families. When we are punished for attempting to be ourselves, we don't grow up to be ourselves. Because we are unhappy with not being ourselves, we look for other ways to become someone. We get stuck with some kind of compulsive behavior. We work too much, drink too much, eat too much, gamble too much, collect too much, talk too much, seek sex too much. An addict is never satisfied. Dysfunctional families are not the only source of addictions, but here is another strong clue you may be able to use.

It is possible you were blamed for all the family's problems. That is a heavy burden. Many who grew up in dysfunctional families accept the guilt, blaming themselves for the fact that Mom could not keep husbands.

This kind of inherited guilt is particularly deep when one has been sexually abused as a child. It is possible to feel more like a participant than a victim. Others may understand that a criminal act has taken place in which the victim had no actual control, but the victim has difficulty seeing it that way.

Breaking the Dysfunctional Chain

One nice thing about growing up is that you can begin to look at your own parents in a new light. You can begin to imagine what it was like when they began dating. They become persons with far more depth and many more facets than you ever perceived as a child. It is even possible to let them attend to their business while you attend to yours.

What you need to escape is co-dependency. There will come a time when you can inform them that you will no longer be responsible for their personal hang-ups and destructive behavior. You were not born to solve their problems. It is possible to live a full life without their blessing. This also applies to your in-laws if you have some who insist on making a mess of their lives. You may have had considerable guilt placed upon your shoulders that is not of your own making. On the other hand, there are numerous other emotional barriers to accepting God's forgiveness, ranging from nagging memories to unpaid debts. Since so many of the remaining obstacles involve other people, we will take a fresh look at some very old, but genuinely helpful, ideas in the next section.

Love does no harm to its neighbor. Therefore love is the fulfillment of the law.
Romans 13:10

Let It Hit Home

☐ Try to imagine what you would have wanted for yourself in a family. What do you think you needed? Can you form an image in your mind of a "Christian home"?

PART FOUR

Ways to Reconciliation

7

It's Between You and Others

He who forgives ends the quarrel.
African proverb

Unresolved conflict will prevent any permanent healing of your wounded conscience. You cannot expect to fully realize God's forgiveness until you have done your best to patch up any damage you may have caused.

Jesus was explicit about this. "If you are offering your gift at the altar and there remember that your brother has something against you, leave your gift there in front of the altar. First go and be reconciled to your brother; then come and offer your gift" (Matthew 5:23-24).

With that terse statement, Jesus exposed one of the most important steps toward forgiving yourself. There is no way around it. The damage you leave unnoticed, unacknowledged, and unrepaired will act like a tourniquet, restricting the flow of God's accepting love.

There is no healthy reason to avoid the facts about what you have done. The very opposite is true. Facing reality and doing all you can to repair the damage you have caused is essential. You can't be helped without this step. Alcoholics Anonymous is emphatic about it. This is a mud puddle you can't go around. It is necessary to make "a list of all persons we [have] harmed, and become willing to make amends to them all . . . [we] cannot remake the present until we undo the past."[15]

Worship activates the conscience. When we are reminded of God, we are simultaneously reminded of our faults. Despite Jesus' love and compassion, he is God. And if he were to suddenly appear at my elbow, I would undoubtedly be overcome with feelings of unworthiness. Like Simon Peter, I could say, "Go away from me, Lord; I am a sinful man!" (Luke 5:8) That must be our starting place with him. The forgiveness will come afterward.

Being "religious," then, does not give us a way to excuse ourselves. We come to God to be set free from sin, not to mask it over. Jesus is not interested in being a spiritual cosmetician. He calls himself a physician. He wants to heal us spiritually.

Making Things Right

At this point in our healing process we must cooperate with God. There is no way we can dodge our responsibility by just going to church. If we have stolen something, we can return it. If we have spoken unkindly, we can apologize. If we have neglected a child, we can get busy and do a better job of being a parent.

I received a long-distance telephone call from a man who had been my neighbor many years before. I do a little woodworking as a hobby, and this man had sold me a certain power tool he no longer needed. I remembered the man and still possess the tool. But I honestly could not remember any of the things he told me about on the phone.

"I feel really bad about it," he said. "I offered you the tool at one price, and when you came to pick it up, I raised it to a higher price."

"I don't remember that," I assured him.

"You told me you didn't have that much money and would have to save some more before you could buy it."

"That sounds like the story of my life," I replied.

"I kept the tool and made you come back later with the higher payment."

I told him that whatever I had paid him must have seemed to me a fair price or I would have resisted. I still had the tool as an important part of my shop equipment and had given the purchase price no further thought.

"But I feel very bad about it," he said, his voice trembling slightly. "I want to mail you the difference."

"No," I insisted. "I have no idea at all what the difference was, and I don't want to be reminded. I am happy with the deal. If you took me for a few bucks it was my fault, not yours."

He continued to press his offer. I finally told him that his phone call was sufficient repayment. It was a beautiful, growing kind of thing that he did. I had forgotten about the incident the day after it happened, and it was time that he forgot about it, too. Eventually, and with indications of relief, we parted good friends.

I wish I knew the rest of his story. Wouldn't it be interesting to know what led him to dial my number and how it has gone with him since? I am cheered by the knowledge that his behavior is a sign of good health. He reminded me of Zacchaeus. After Jesus had been the house guest of this tax collector from Jericho, Zacchaeus said, "Look Lord! Here and now I give half of my possessions to the poor, and if I have cheated anybody out of anything, I will pay back four times the amount." Jesus said to him, "Today salvation has come to this house . . ." (Luke 19:8-9).

The formal label of this action is *restitution*—restoring something to its rightful owner or somehow making up a loss that cannot be recovered. In other words, doing everything you can to make things right again.

Penance is another term the church has sometimes used. It is a very good word to keep in our vocabulary, but it is also prone to distortion. It can go beyond simple repayment, or even enthusiastic generosity, and become an act of self-abasement performed with the desire to somehow pay for sin. Remind yourself that Christ has already paid the bill, canceling your debt. He has no desire to see you mortified and humiliated.

On the other hand, making restitution admits your responsibility. You share the cost of your sin. Doing everything you can to make amends will not only bring you great relief, it will also help keep you out of the same trouble again.

Some Helpful Suggestions

You have been unable to forgive yourself. You are feeling guilty because you know you have done something wrong. Others may have encouraged you and do not accuse you. But you accuse yourself. You are certain your behavior is an offense before God. You have frankly admitted it, and you believe God forgives you. Now you want to make amends. You want to fix what you have already messed up and try to do better tomorrow. What can you do? What are some valid ways of "making restitution" or "doing penance" in these modern times?

Although much may depend upon your particular religious beliefs, I have no doubt that the simple suggestions presented here will be compatible with your faith.

A telephone call. I have already shown you how this can work. The telephone is an amazing instrument. It can get people together over tremendous distances at low cost. With satellite technology at your disposal, you can tell someone in another hemisphere you are sorry, person-to-person. Your feeling will be conveyed in a direct manner that is disarming. There are very few nasty people who will not accept an apology. You may be amazed at how quickly a festering sore can be removed.

Whether or not the other person will meet you halfway makes little difference. You will have done your part. Call that other person now. Say you are sorry and want to do what you can to restore things to the way they were before.

A letter. Sometimes writing a letter can be better than making a phone call. The beauty of a letter is that it doesn't force the other person to respond immediately. If the offended party is really put out with you, there may be a fiery exchange that will do more harm than good. An emotional response like that is almost uncontrollable if the problem is a painful one. You may not get to first base. A letter stands a better chance of giving you the opportunity to express yourself. The recipient's response may be hostile at first, but after a time of reflection on your apparent sincerity, a little softening is likely.

Fancy letter writing is a lost art. And that's a good thing! You don't want to send anything that looks even slightly phony. Be honest. Tell the other person you are hurting because you have hurt him. It doesn't take two pages to say you are sorry.

A gift. Here is a classic way of doing indirect penance! Many jokes have been told about the traveling salesman bringing home something from the airport gift shop. And yet there is something nice about a little present given as a peace offering. It can open the way to healthy conversation. It can do the job as a silent symbol. Don't overdo it. Don't underdo it. Make it thoughtful. If it can have some connection (humorous or serious) with the problem, so much the better.

A visit. Few things are more effective than going out of your way to ask for forgiveness. Whether you travel across the country or around the block makes little difference. The important thing is that you care enough to stand face-to-face with the other person and express yourself. If the other person is hostile and angry, remain civil. Say you are sorry and desire to make amends. If your offer is rejected and you are thrown out of the house, at least you have done all you can. Your expression of regret will probably go a long way toward restoring harmony even though your relationship may remain somewhat strained for a while.

A phone call in advance of such a visit is always in order. If you catch the other person at an inconvenient (or embarrassing) moment, you will do your cause no good. Make sure you will be welcomed before you ring the doorbell.

A prayer. Perhaps circumstances absolutely rule out any of the ideas above. Maybe you don't know where to find the other person, or perhaps much time has passed and you have lost all connection with the locality and people involved in the misdeed that still brings you grief. You can say a prayer for them. Prayer knows no limit of time or place. It can reach out in arms of strength and healing from wherever you are. Ask God to help you make it up to them. Pray his blessing upon them even as you seek forgiveness for yourself.

There are some other ways of getting the job done, of course. Some of them are quite direct and to the point. (Did you steal a chicken? Return two chickens!) Others are more subtle and indirect. (Did you hurt a child ten years ago? Send her to college today!) Moreover, these things are not to be done independently but in appropriate combinations. (Pray, make a phone call, take a gift during a visit, pray some more!)

What I have tried to do is stir your imagination a little. There are no hard and fast rules at this point. Don't let anyone impose them on you. There is no book worth consulting that will list a specific price of penance to offset a particular sin. The Pharisees of this world have been writing such books for centuries. But human relations and matters of the heart cannot be dealt with like a flat-rate manual (the mechanic's guide to auto repair). You alone know what is best, what is appropriate. The important thing is to understand that something needs to be done. You have a responsibility to try to straighten out whatever is wrong between yourself and others.

Get rid of all bitterness, rage and anger, brawling and slander, along with every form of malice. Be kind and compassionate to one another, forgiving each other, just as in Christ God forgave you.
Ephesians 4:31-32

Let It Hit Home

☐ Recall a major conflict you have had in the past that was resolved. How did the reconciliation come about?

☐ Recall a conflict in your life that has not been resolved. Why has reconciliation not occurred?

8

Forgiving Yourself

*In the sphere of forgiveness, too many
hatchets are buried alive.*
Lem Hubard, *The Chicago Tribune*

You are facing a fork in the road. Now you must
decide which way you will go. You will turn your back
on one way and travel the other. The choice will be
yours, but you will go on. There can be no turning
back.

In an earlier chapter we saw how repression spares
us many painful memories. Unfortunately, this
psychological mechanism is highly selective. Most
often you are left with a lot to think about. The final
step in forgiving yourself is to find a way to turn these
memories over to God. Continuing to kick yourself is
not the answer. Brooding over the past is exhausting,
not productive.

There is a lesson in China's *Hsiao Ching* that deals
with mourning the death of one's parents. In many
ways, forgiving yourself parallels the process of grief.

When mourning, a son weeps without wailing . . .
He speaks without rhetorical flourish; he feels uncomfortable in fine clothing; he feels no joy on hear-

ing music; he does not relish food—all this is in the nature of grief. After three days he breaks his fast to show men that the dead should not hurt the living and that disfigurement should not lead to the destruction of life—this is the rule of the sages.[16]

Regret is both helpful and harmful. If being sorry for your behavior increases your desire to live a more orderly life, thank God for the birth pangs. But if you begin to feel so much regret that it makes you despondent, watch out! If you can find no comfort anywhere, no hope for tomorrow, and become sloppy in your work and recreation, then your awareness of sin is no longer your servant. You have become its slave.

So much happiness, your own and that of others, depends upon your choice at this point. The only help I can offer is of a religious nature. I believe forgiving yourself is a theological problem. Maybe you don't consider yourself particularly religious. Perhaps you go to church on Christmas and Easter, or only at weddings and funerals. Maybe your mind is too occupied with business and sports to have much room left for divine contemplation.

My friend, you need God. If you have stuck with me this far, don't turn away now. I promise to keep my feet planted squarely on earth. No make-believe. No signs and wonders. No silly word games. Nothing but open honesty about a healthy relationship that can be built between you and God.

One reminder: Don't jump in here. Everything contained in the earlier chapters is vital preparation for this final step. If you randomly turned to these pages, be sure to go back and read the others.

Positive Ways to Recovery

The suggestions that follow are simple, but you may not find them easy. Think them through as you read. Slow your pace. Reflect upon each idea. At the end of each suggestion is a portion of a prayer that is written as a letter to God. Try to really pray as you read. These words can become your prayer as you reflect upon each possibility. If this is your personal copy, take time to write your responses in each blank. If you are concerned about someone else seeing what you have written, make your notations in a code of your own invention. Just jot down initials, or a word that summarizes what you are thinking.

1. Thank God for the hurt. Does your feeling of guilt increase your sensitivity to others? Are you more aware of God than before? Have you come face-to-face with yourself in a new way? Wonderful! These are all good things. This is your opportunity to stop putting up false fronts. Now you can have a little more sympathy for the other hurt souls. Best of all, you are aware of your imperfection. Because of your painful memories you may not be content with solo work from here on. God's plow has turned your garden. Thank him for it.

Dear God,
It is not easy to be thankful for the way I have been feeling. You know how low I have been. Help me now to use this difficult time of my life as a springboard to something better.
    I list here the names of anyone I can remember hurting:

_____

_____

_____

_____

_____

_____

2. Determine whether the guilt you feel is authentic or counterfeit. Face it. A lot of misery is caused by unrealistic standards. If you exaggerate the thing beyond all reasonable proportions, your guilt can become neurotic. Counterfeit guilt is generated by the imagination. It makes the proverbial mountain out of a molehill. Some slight social *faux pas* becomes inflated beyond its actual significance. Parents (bless 'em!) are experts at creating guilt-inducing tensions.

I have already castigated irresponsible clergy. Let me add well-meaning teachers to the list. Friends often set artificial standards of dress and behavior. The things such people have made you feel bad about may be nothing but trifles. Don't let anyone but God set the gauge on your conscience.

Authentic guilt accompanies actual wrongdoing. It is the price you pay for being human. You recognize your responsibility without evasion. This is the guilt Christ can relieve.

Help me to sort things out, O God. I am confused. There are so many rules I don't understand. I no longer trust my conscience. Sometimes it remains silent when I am doing something terrible. Sometimes it bothers me when I am merely enjoying myself.

_____ By checking this blank, I promise to become more familiar with the rules as you have given them in the Bible. I want to know more clearly what is right and what is wrong in your sight.

3. Be sorry for the right thing. The thing most people regret is that they got caught. According to many, cheating may be a crime, but reporting it is far worse.

My wife, Anna, once received an irate telephone call from a stranger. The woman was angry to the point of breathlessness. "I want to thank your husband for getting me in trouble."

Anna did not know how to respond. She may have gurgled a little, "What?"

"He turned me in to the game warden. I got a ticket for trout fishing."

Since I was not at home, Anna had to deal with this one the best way she could. She said she had not heard anything about it from me.

"Well, he did. And him a preacher!"

Anna told me about it when I returned home. Because the woman sounded so distraught and threatening, I thought it advisable to check with the game warden. He told me that several people had been cited for fishing in a newly stocked stream before the season opened. Both of us agreed that I had nothing to do with any of the situations. In fact, I had not been near a trout stream that month.

The matter remained a mystery for almost a year. Then at a covered-dish dinner in a neighboring church, I heard another pastor tell the most interesting personal anecdote. He said he had been visiting a certain member who lived by a trout stream when he saw a shiny new fish stringer in a public trash can. He praised his good luck and lifted it out. To his astonishment, three beautiful rainbow trout were attached—still kicking. Then he saw the game warden who was asking a woman if they were hers. She admitted they were and so he wrote her a ticket. The pastor thought this an extremely funny story. And thus I began to understand vicarious suffering.

Being sorry you got caught is not as helpful as being sorry you made a poor choice.

You are my friend, O Lord. You know it is easier for me to regret discovery more than my behavior. You were there when I stole something, sneaked a little, fudged on a report, broke some laws, or did something else I regret.
I recall such times right now.

_____

_____

_____

_____

_____

_____

4. Be open and receptive. Christ called the Holy Spirit "the Comforter" (John 14:26, KJV). An interesting title. The Greek word involved is *paraclete.* Literally it means "one called to the side of." It could be translated "Counselor" or "Helper." If you cooperate with God's Spirit, you may be led to understand yourself more fully. As the hurt is revealed to you, you will take tremendous strides forward in your spiritual maturity.

A woman berated her minister for using the word "alcoholic" in the pulpit. A man became unusually distressed when he saw one four-year-old punch another in the solar plexis. We need not be famous psychologists to understand the principle involved in these examples. It is almost impossible, however, to be objective when it comes to understanding ourselves. If we are open and receptive, the Holy Spirit will reveal what is hidden.

O Lord, I am not totally familiar with spiritual things. I am not sure what is being asked of me here. There are some aspects of this that trouble me:

_____

_____

_____

_____

_____

At the same time, I also understand the potential good that could come into my life with your Spirit. Help me now to open the doors of my being to your Holy Presence.

Check each item below as you are able to pray it truthfully:

_____ I open the door of doubt.

_____ I open the door of hesitancy.

_____ I open the door of aloofness.

_____ I open the door of self-sufficiency.

_____ I open the door of regret.

_____ I open the door of jealousy.

_____ I open the door of shame.

_____ Come, Holy Spirit, dwell within me.

5. Look at the offense with Christ. Now we come to the pinnacle. You may think there is not enough oxygen up here for you. Don't turn away. Remember, I promised to keep my feet planted firmly on earth. What I am recommending is that you "return to the scene of the crime," as it were, and take Christ with you. Think of it as a child holding an adult's hand in the dark. There may be something there you don't want to see. Examine it in the bright light of Christ's presence. Let him show you what is good in it. Notice that he does not become hysterical. He is not critical and squeamish. He does not pound you on the head with a Bible and ask you why you couldn't have done better. He puts his arm around you. Yes, it is a mess. But how can it be used to help you?

Joseph's jealous brothers sold him into slavery. Later, when his presence in Egypt meant food for his starving family, he was able to say to them, "You intended to harm me, but God intended it for good to accomplish what is now being done, the saving of many lives" (Genesis 50:20).

Did you see any of the photographs of Pope John Paul II's visit to the jail cell of Mehmet Ali Agca? Agca was the man who attempted to assassinate the Pope. There they were together, victim and would-be murderer. The conversation was private. We can be sure our subject was discussed. In that exchange you can see Christ at work. Without hesitation, take Christ back with you in your mind. Let him hear everything, see everything.

Lord, if I had lived when you walked in Galilee, would I have wanted to be near you? Would I have been as attracted to you as all those other people were? If we had engaged in private conversation, would you have made me feel uncomfortable or welcomed? I am sure you would have seen through all my false fronts. You would have quickly gone right to the heart of who I am. Would that have scared me, Lord? Would I have been nervous when I was talking with you?

As I read the Gospels I see only the self-righteous, the pretenders getting uneasy when you were with them. You were warm and gracious to sinners like me. Help me to understand that's still the way it is. Let me feel your arm around me now. Come back with me to the time when things like these happened:

_____

_____

_____

_____

_____

_____

_____

_____

What do you see, Jesus? Is there something I am missing? Is there any hope for me? I will pause, right now, and look at this mess with you. Let's stay here together a while . . .

_____

_____

_____

_____

_____

_____

_____

6. Replace regret with love. A part of your inability to forgive yourself is nothing more than anger and resentment toward others. It is even likely that you are trying to hurt someone else by hurting yourself. Ask God to help you get rid of negative feelings. He can replace them with something much more constructive—love. Love for others. Love for God. Love for yourself.

It is no secret to you, O God. You know how I feel. You know the truth behind my attitude this moment. Lead me now to know myself. What is it I really want to accomplish by feeling the way I feel? Why do I cherish such thoughts? How can anything so bitter be a comfort to me?

Now help me to love _____.

And _____.

And _____.

It won't be easy. I truly need your help. Let this become possible for me, Lord.

7. Change your life. As you make new choices, remember that forgiving yourself is not a one-time change in attitude—it requires a change in your actions. Beating yourself is nothing more than an attempt to put off self-discipline and service to others. The Christ who unfailingly forgave sin never once told the sinner to keep it up. Jesus asked the woman caught in adultery, "Woman, where are they? Has no one condemned you?" "No one, sir," she said. "Then neither do I condemn you," Jesus declared. "Go now and leave your life of sin" (John 8:10-11).

You must live out your forgiveness every day. As long as you continue stumbling over the same familiar stone, you will never feel better about yourself. Melvin Konner has pointed out that there are biological constraints on the human spirit. We do many things because we are genetically programmed to feel everything from rage to lust to gluttony.[17] But I have seen too many lives made new to consider the situation hopeless. We can change our actions. It is never too late to start again.

If I could name one thing I never want to do again, it is:

_____

_____

_____

_____

_____

_____

_____

That one behavior is a great burden to me and to others. Put a power in me, God, that will stop it. I don't want to go on repeating myself in this.

Of course I am not a person with only one fault. These things also grieve me about myself:

Let me start anew. From this moment forward, let me be a changed person. Let my mistakes be new mistakes. Let my problems be fresh problems. Don't let me go on and on in the same old way.

8. Follow your own insights. By now, you may have thought of something that could help. Pause a day or an hour, and it may slip away from you. Capitalize upon it. Is there some specific detail that needs the application of your time and energy? If so, get to it. Today is better than tomorrow.

In the presence of God, understanding that he is merciful, I confess the sin I hate and humbly ask for pardon. This is the only hope I have. I make a vow of faith. I renounce all evil. To God I dedicate my mind, my heart, my body. If I should give in to temptation and fail to keep this strong resolve, I will, with the help of the Holy Spirit, stop as soon as I see what is happening and return to God for mercy without delay.

This is my desire and my resolution. I sign it now without reservation or exception.

_____

(signed)

Dear Lord, help me to keep this sacrifice of my heart. As you have inspired me to do this, give me the strength to keep it. Amen.

If you have worked through your feelings this far, you have come a long way. You are still not home free. You have more to do. Being human, you will stumble again. There is no pessimism in that statement. It is an acknowledgment of fact. Accepting God's forgiveness and forgiving yourself will not suddenly make you perfect. Someday take the time to read about the people we call "saints." You will be astonished by their struggles and blemished records. You are no different from anyone else. Now you need to get ready for next time.

If God is for us, who can be against us? He who did not spare his own Son, but gave him up for us all—how will he not also, along with him, graciously give us all things? Who will bring any charge against those whom God has chosen? It is God who justifies. Who is he that condemns? Christ Jesus, who died—more than that, who was raised to life—is at the right hand of God and is also interceding for us. Who shall separate us from the love of Christ?
Romans 8:31b-35a

Let It Hit Home

❏ Where are you in this eight-step process of recovery?

❏ What actions will you take to get to the next step?

PART FIVE

Preparing for the Rest of Your Life

9

Spiritual Preparation for Next Time

To repent is to alter one's way of looking at life; it is to take God's point of view instead of one's own.
Anonymous

With confession we begin our journey. When we understand that our Creator's attitude toward us is kind, we quicken our pace. By sincerely doing everything we can to repair as much of our damage as possible, we approach our goal. Perfection, our journey's end, will have to wait for heaven. Even if we make a dramatic change or experience religious conversion, we will probably swap one set of temptations for another. More occasions for personal disappointment and grief are surely coming. "Sin is crouching at your door; it desires to have you, but you must master it" (Genesis 4:7b).

Cultivate Your Spirit

Nothing will help you master yourself better than careful attention to your spiritual life. God gave you the facility, but you are responsible to develop it. All of us have muscles, but athletes condition theirs beyond the ordinary. Through exercise and training they develop different sets of muscles for their particular sport. A weight lifter is not the best boxer. A runner does not have a lineman's neck. In the same way, we can refine our spirit to fit our place in life. It is a mistake to assume that the ultimate spiritual life is that of a monk in a monastery. That is best for *him.* The devout life can be lived anywhere. You are not required to withdraw from ordinary life. The human soul is flexible. It will expand to fill an infinite variety of lives.

Fortunately, we have some excellent guidance available. Most churches today have someone who can give you spiritual direction. However, it is not all of the same caliber. Shop around until you find a congregation whose public worship reaches you. It may or may not be the most popular place in town. God has been known to use third-rate preaching in a powerful way. The important thing is for the style and content to be in harmony with your soul. Do the prayers, hymns, selections of Scripture, and comments touch anywhere near your wavelength? People are different. Churches are different. If all you get are answers to questions you never ask, you are sitting in the wrong pew. Somewhere, you will find a church in harmony with your soul. That is where you belong.

Possibly the only spiritual guidance you will need can be gathered through regular involvement in such a church. If you want to dig still deeper, you will find the minister eager to talk with you. Don't be hesitant about asking for a personal conversation. Any pastor who is not sidetracked by ecclesiastical politics will be eager to hear from you.

As an adult, I attempted to learn to play the piano. I bought a used piano and had it delivered to my apartment. Night after night I practiced diligently. My choice of music was necessarily limited to the little pieces children use to get started.

After a month or two of this, I discovered that my next-door neighbor was a music instructor for the city schools. I was mortified! The walls were thin. I knew he had been hearing me. My desire was to play Bach, but I was restricted to songs entitled "The Dancing Elephant" and "Butterfly Waltz." Do you know what I did? I stopped practicing. I was ashamed to let a genuine musician hear a grown man stumble through sixteen measures of five-finger exercises.

Now I understand it differently. My neighbor may have been delighted with my attempt. His entire life was dedicated to bringing music into people's lives. It probably cheered him to see an adult taking the plunge. Think how much he could have taught me! I imagine every time I hit a B natural instead of a B flat he wanted to rush over and tell me how to get it right. I was living next to a gold mine of assistance. All I needed to do was ask. Instead, I chose the losing way. I withdrew in embarrassment.

Don't let it happen to you. If you feel the slightest twitch of life in your soul, seek an opportunity to talk it over with someone who can guide you along the way. You will be welcomed if you are sincere. Being a beginner has nothing to do with it. Jesus said there will be rejoicing in heaven when you get started on your way.

Read, Listen, Look

Without question, the greatest spiritual treasury we have is the Bible. Get one in a clear, modern translation and read it regularly. You will also need some guidance here. The Bible is a big book. Almost a million words. I mean nothing disrespectful when I tell you it is an uneven collection. There are pages that will lift your spirit into the holy presence of God. There are other pages that will perplex and annoy you. God can teach you something through all of it, but in the beginning you need to be selective. If you start reading with Genesis, page one, you are not likely to survive through Leviticus. At least not at first. Eventually, after you have learned enough about the Bible and biblical history, you may read it cover-to-cover in several versions and enjoy every minute of it.

Where should you start? If you have a minute or two, turn to the Psalms. They are habit-forming. They record every up and down of the human soul. In just a few lines you will find an expression of the very things you feel. Turn to them at random and try a few. You will be amazed at how reading one leads to another. I have found them so helpful that I regret there are only one hundred fifty of them. One of the best ways to learn to pray is to pray the Psalms.

If you want to know about Jesus, read one of the first four books of the New Testament—Matthew, Mark, Luke, or John. These four Gospels are the only source of information we have about Christ's ministry. Even though they all tell the same story, they tell it differently. Each author had a particular "angle," a special way of looking at Jesus. For the complete picture, you will need to read all four. Mark is written the earliest. It is also the shortest. I heard it recited aloud by an actor in less than two hours (including intermission). You can read it silently in less time than it would take you to watch a movie.

The letters of Paul have been well served by modern translations. Because they are letters, you need to familiarize yourself with a little bit of history. Some Bibles have short introductions printed before each book. There are dozens of good commentaries available.

The Bible is God's way of revealing himself to us. He speaks through a variety of human personalities over a wide span of years, but there is a unity in what is being said. Read it all. If you are not excited by the fact that Buz was the brother of Uz, skip a page now and then. The blessings will flow in direct proportion to your familiarity with Scripture.

There is other good reading you can do. Through the centuries we have inherited a priceless collection of devotional literature. These books will never go out of print. They will continue to instruct souls until the end of time. Here are a few that have meant a lot to me.

St. Augustine, *Confessions.* The first nine "books" (chapters) of this spiritual gem tell an unforgettable true story of the author's personal spiritual struggle. He tells it all. His handicaps were both those of a skeptical mind and the passions of the flesh. The description of his ultimate conversion is as exciting a passage of autobiography as you will ever find. Augustine is breathless in places, and you will be too. I cannot overstate its value. But do try to find a twentieth-century translation.[18] Older renderings tend to make him stuffy.

The Imitation of Christ. Ordinarily attributed to Thomas à Kempis, the authorship of this famous work is still being debated. With a series of very brief lessons, it teaches the basics of applied Christianity. The comments are honest, to the point, and counter to popular thinking. You will receive jolt upon jolt as you read. The arrogant and proud are simply sliced to ribbons. But like the cat that first bites and then licks the wounded flesh, the *Imitation* brings a special kind of salve to your soul. Its comments regarding humility are beyond parallel. You will disagree with some of its contents, but you will be hard-pressed to win the opposing side of the debate.

Don't read this one when you are too young to profit from it. Or if you do, be sure to come back to it again in your middle years. The profundity of its simple insights will make you gasp aloud. Like *Confessions*, this great devotional classic will be most helpful in a modern reinterpretation.[19]

Brother Lawrence, *The Practice of the Presence of God.* This little book is a collection of conversations and letters by a seventeenth-century kitchen helper, Nicholas Herman. He relates how God is intimately present at every moment and every place, and how we can be constantly aware of him. His perpetual state of worship may seem a bit strange to you at first. Eventually, you will see the value of doing even small things for the love of God. Again, you will find a modern reinterpretation extremely helpful![20]

Thomas Kelly, *A Testament of Devotion.*[21] Among books written in this century, this one stands supreme. Here is a serious, credible attempt to bring honest spirituality into focus today. To read this Quaker's call to obedience is to confront inescapable truth. It is a shining jewel from the first page to the last.

Remember that your eyes can be used for looking as well as for reading. If the only Christian art you have seen is Sunday school leaflets, try visiting a museum or check out a book of paintings from your library. Many of the greatest art treasures have a religious theme. Examine the paintings of the Sistine Chapel again, not as a curious student, but as a devout soul. If you ever visit St. Peter's, stand still for ten minutes or so before Michelangelo's *Pieta.*

Let your ears help you cultivate your spirit. The catalog of inspirational music is vast. It includes compositions by the masters and contemporary music of great warmth. Have you experienced the forgiveness of God and truly forgiven yourself? Then the next time you stand for Handel's "Hallelujah Chorus" from *The Messiah,* let his music express your joy.

One of my favorites is Bach, *The Passion According to Saint Matthew.* Few musical compositions are more evocative of mental pictures. The opening measures sweep the listener away. You are suddenly there, standing by the dusty road where Jesus is being led to Calvary. Each footstep is in the music. The swirling movement of the orchestra reflects our own dismay at seeing this terrible procession. It never lets up. You will weep with Peter in his denial, cringe with every stinging stroke of the lash on Christ's bare back, wait in silent faith before a freshly sealed tomb. I am drawn back to this amazing composition every Easter season. It is no exaggeration when I say Bach transports me. I can say, "I was there when they crucified my Lord."

There are many other classical and contemporary works fully deserving of hours of concentrated, active listening. If they seem alien to you now, believe me—

they will grow on you. Give them a chance. You will be glad you did.

Combine your ears and eyes to deepen your spiritual life through poetry. Poets tell us things about the ways of God with a soul that cannot be expressed in prose. Rediscover religious poetry. Yes, a lot of it is maudlin, but there is enough first-class verse to offset it. Perhaps the time has come to tackle one of the long poems of Milton, Wordsworth, or Dante.

If such works are not suited to your taste, get a book of popular, contemporary religious verse or prose. Books of poetic narrative such as Calvin Miller's trilogy (*The Singer, The Song,* and *The Finale*) say things that will sear your heart in a few lines.[22] Another inspirational book that will stop you in your tracks is *Ragman and Other Cries of Faith* by Walter Wangerin, Jr.[23]

Almost anything by the prolific authors Henri Nouwen or Frederick Buechner is worth your time.

Prayer

The best way to cultivate your spiritual life, by far, is private prayer. People are forever saying they don't know how to pray. What do they mean? Is there some trick to it, some mysterious technique they need to learn before they can attempt it? No way! It is as natural as breathing. In fact, one of the earliest popular prayers of the church is the Jesus Prayer: "Lord Jesus Christ, Son of God; have mercy on me, a sinner." This prayer is intended to be prayed as we breathe. On the first phrase we inhale; on the second we exhale. A little book from early Russia, *The Way of a Pilgrim*, recounts the remarkable results of praying the Jesus Prayer without ceasing.[24]

To be sure, not all prayer is of equal depth. The important thing is to talk with God and tell him what concerns you. Ask for guidance. Remember others. Always be honest—you are not praying if you pretend. God knows your heart.

Take courage here from the prayers of the Bible. Job cursed the day he was born. Jeremiah is in a rage over the personal pain resulting from his reluctant but inescapable prophesying. Some of the Psalms, like Dante, delight in imagining what God will do to one's enemies. You may not find such prayers "inspirational," but God welcomes them. Why? Because they are truthful. They expose the soul. It is only when we are open and honest that God can work in us. If your first prayers are full of complaint and whining, your later ones will make up for it.

Earlier I suggested that you write God a letter. If you are sure you can keep such things private, this is a marvelous approach to prayer. As they accumulate over a period of years you will be able to dig back through them and find value for your soul that otherwise would have been lost. John Baillie's *A Diary of Private Prayer* is a classic aid that has remained in print for more than thirty years.[25] New prayer guides are published every year.

Groups

You will find a special kind of support in the right group. You were cautioned earlier about the dangers inherent in becoming a part of the wrong group. Only you can decide which is which, and you can do that only after repeated exposure. It is worth the effort to find a healthy group of people who are studying the Scriptures and praying together.

Guilt, shame, and hurt prosper like mushrooms in dark and moldy places. Fresh air and sunshine have a way of cleansing us. If you sit alone and nurse your feelings they will get worse. When you get around others who have a positive outlook, such feelings seem to dissolve. If you experience the genuine love and acceptance of a Christian study or prayer group you will be blessed. In the right kind of small group you will discover that people do not reject you because of the things that trouble you. They will be responding to you the same way Christ responded to the people with problems he met along the way. They understand that finger wagging and verbal reprimands are not what you need. You are already doing enough of that for yourself. Instead, they will share a journey of faith with you. Everyone present will undoubtedly know what it is to accept God's forgiveness. You may even find someone who has had feelings similar to your own.

There is something in prayer and Bible study with others that will open new windows for you. Ask around. You will find some that meet in churches, some that meet in homes, and some that gather for breakfast or lunch at a neighborhood restaurant. You will undoubtedly be welcomed. I never yet saw a Christian group that wasn't eager to receive new faces. Your arrival will validate the authenticity of what they are trying to do. Don't hesitate to ask if you can become a part of it.

If you want to be ready for the next time of temptation or uncontrollable reflex, begin now to cultivate your spiritual life. It is your best insurance against falling over that same stone.

> How can a young man keep his way pure? By living according to your word. . . . I have hidden your word in my heart that I might not sin against you.
> *Psalm 119:9, 11*

Let It Hit Home

☐ What reaches you with the most force? Poetry? Music? Books? Visual arts?

☐ Make a note of at least one spiritual discipline you will embark upon during the next month. Tie that discipline into the answer you gave to the above question.

10

Emotional Preparation for Next Time

Repentance may begin instantly, but reformation often requires a sphere of years.
Henry Ward Beecher

Tears and laughter are an important part of life. They are special gifts. Releasing your emotions today will make a difference in how you feel tomorrow.

Boys were told, "Men don't cry." With the movement toward equality of the sexes, this idea is expanding. Someday someone will say it is inhuman to cry. The taut faces of young people are symptoms of an emotion-repressing generation. The desire is to appear neither hurting nor happy. It is certainly defensive. Are you a teenager? You hurt, don't you? Is it that you don't want others to see your pain? Is that why you scowl? I see your frozen faces in advertising, on music videos, and in every school. What are you saying? I think I know. "Dear Mom, Dad, so-called friends, community—you can't say you've destroyed me if I don't shed any tears."

Putting our emotions on hold is like pausing to look at a frame on a VCR. You can do it for a little while, but if you continue something is going to go wrong. You can chew up your insides the same way you can chew up a VHS tape. "When we bottle up feelings . . . it is the same as starting the timer of a time bomb . . . The longer the time bomb ticks, the closer it comes to an explosion."[26] The longer you refuse to express your emotions, the closer you come to genuine trouble for yourself and others.

Cultivate Your Emotions

At any age, to refuse to cry is to be less than human. Even animals without tear ducts have been observed in what appears to be grief responses. If you want to purge your soul, have a good cry. Do it in private, if you must, but do it. It will dissolve some of that wall you have built around yourself.

If your problem is turning off the tears you may need another kind of help. None of the above applies to you. But read on.

Laughter is closely related to tears. It is equally effective as a tension reliever. Laughing does good things for the soul. Sometimes we take ourselves too seriously. If you cultivate your sense of humor until it can include a few chuckles at your own expense, you will have grown spiritually.

The humor I am speaking of results from a philosophical perspective on the ups and downs of daily life. Tragedy and comedy are often separated only by our perception of the situation. I will give you one more example from my own life.

The occasion was a gathering of Presbyterians, including some of the highest dignitaries, at the denomination's state conference grounds in Virginia. I had been asked to show one of my home movies for the evening program. The film was new and still needed a little narration to be complete, but I thought, "No problem, I'll take the microphone and finish the soundtrack before dinner."

The first bad omen came when we discovered I had left my wallet at home in another pair of trousers. Dinner would be on the house, but we did think it prudent that my wife Anna drive.

When we arrived at that Presbyterian haven, I explained that I needed a quiet place for an hour or so and was given a private room on the hotel's second floor. I took my equipment up and then drove Anna, our children and my visiting mother to nearby Lake Shenandoah so they could have an outing while I worked. I had brought along a little boat on the top of my car—a kit-built kayak. In a few minutes I had launched the boat, instructed the children to be courteous to the lone fisherman on the dock, and returned to my makeshift movie studio. The distance was short, so I took the risk of driving without a license in my pocket.

By five o'clock, an hour before dinner, I had successfully completed the narration of about half the film. Then it broke. "No problem," I thought. "I'll slip into Harrisonburg and buy some splicing tapes." Without a wallet, I had only the change in my pocket: 70 cents.

It wasn't enough. They had been priced for the Bicentennial: 76 cents plus tax. Dinner was in forty-five minutes, but I remained calmly confident that I could finish the job in time for the 7:30 showing. So I drove to pick up my family. They would have some money.

The children had tied the boat to the end of the dock. I decided it would be easier to take it out if I paddled it over to where the car was parked. When I stepped in, my foot came down outside the center of gravity, and the boat rocked a little. I began to lose my balance. In a quick reflex, my other foot shot out to catch me. It landed on that stick the plans referred to as the "gunwale." With that, the whole thing took the smoothest, quietest, fastest flip imaginable, and I was totally under water, my shoulder in the muddy bottom.

With some effort, I got my feet down and stood up in chest-deep water, the keel of the overturned boat before me. Two members of my family looked stunned, two were laughing, and one was crying. Br'er Bangley, he lay low. I stood there trying to fathom the situation. I could feel the ooze creeping into my shoes. Anna insists that my first words were: "And this isn't my greatest problem."

Having proved that my boat would still float fully loaded with water, I had to face the fact that I was the guest of honor at a dinner due to begin in twenty-five minutes. I would soon be the center of attention for a crowd of my peers that included top-ranking officials. We pooled all the cash at our disposal. Twenty-two dollars and change. I decided to buy some dry clothes. Letting Anna drive, we deposited my mother and the children at the hotel, asked them to hold our seats at the dinner table, and went to a nearby K-Mart. My shoes began to smell exactly like the bottom of a two-year-old aquarium. There was no way to try anything on. I was dripping all over the floor. Anything I touched would be ruined. So I bought sizes larger than usual in case they had been cut on the tight side. I found trousers, underwear, a pullover shirt, socks, and a pair of $4.95 shoes made in Mexico. Adding a 76-cent package of splicing tape, I headed for the checkout counter and told Anna to pull the car up to the front door. We still had five minutes. The girl rang up each item, totalled them, and added tax. You guessed it! $24.38.

"I'm sorry," I said, "I don't have enough money. We'll have to take something out." It occurred to me that of all the items on the counter that would bring the total under twenty-two dollars, there was only one thing that could be sacrificed with no one noticing the difference.

I dashed back to the hotel, rinsed off as much lake bottom as possible, dressed in my baggy new clothing, and marched into the dining room as though nothing had happened. After the film and some friendly compliments, I mentioned to the manager that I had had a little accident and had used his towels. "Nothing serious, I hope?"

"No," I replied, "Nothing serious."

Other examples abound. The Associated Press reported the story of a man who had received a "good smile" from a woman in a bar. He took her to his place. She mixed the drinks, spiking his with a knock-out drug. When he woke, he found his apartment ransacked and his valuables stolen. What did he have to say about the episode? "We guys are jerks. We are stupid, dumb."[27] That's a mixture of tears and laughter.

As We Part

Have you talked to God about your life? Have you tried to set straight what you made crooked? Have you quit? Then forget about it. Turn it over to God. Accept his assurance of pardon. Say with Joseph, "God has made me forget all my trouble . . ." (Genesis 41:51b). Anything more than this is a complete waste of your time and energy. Continuing to wonder whether or not you have committed an unforgivable sin is an indication of spiritual sickness. With God's loving arms around you, get on with your life and work.

You may stumble again as soon as you put this book down. Don't let it shake your confidence in God. Return to him again and again, after every defeat. Don't allow anything to separate you from his love. Eventually, things will improve. You will begin to trust your own willpower less and God more. You will increasingly dislike whatever it is that tempts you. Pray little prayers along the way.

"Lord, when I try to do it myself I make a mess of it."

"O God, it would have been worse than that if you had not prevented me."

"Help me to offend you less tomorrow, my Lord." Think more about God and less about your weakness.

From now on, choose carefully what you put into your memory. You have a clean diary, a new beginning. Some events in your life will come unbidden and will be largely beyond your control, but your response to them will be of your own making.

Consider what so many have reported—that flashing discharge of memory in the face of death quite as though it had all been stored on magnetic tape. One of the most important selections you will ever make is choosing which pictures to hang upon the walls of your mind.

Living a forgiven life is an experience of freedom and joy beyond comparison. It improves your relationships with others, enhances your communion with God, and strengthens your confidence in yourself. Anything you gain by refusing to forgive yourself is certainly far less desirable.

Try to get started. Even a small step is important if you take it in the right direction. The significant thing is not so much how far you have distanced yourself from the pain of guilt as it is which direction you are headed. If you continue to wallow in self-recrimination you are going down. This is not a movement-free idling. Before you put this book down, make a promise to yourself that you will turn the corner. There will be no puff of smoke or flash of light that will suddenly make everything OK. But if you are determined to move in a positive direction you are on the way to healing. At the very least, say to yourself, "Enough of this! Sure, I am a complex person. Maybe only God understands me. But with God's help I can set myself on a more positive, healthier course. I will at least set my direction toward a happier acceptance of myself."

Making that kind of resolution will require you to also accept the facts about your past behavior. Things are the way they are. There is no guessing about that. The things you have done, as well as the things you have failed to do, exist as a record that can't be erased. You can't change any of that. It's either done or it's not done. The only thing you can do is accept it as fact.

While you are at it, accept your own humanity as a given fact. To be human is to be filled with tremendous potential. It is also to be less than perfect. This is the time to get rid thoughts such as, "I should," "I ought," or "I must." These can be damaging notions. Remember the struggle Saint Paul had trying to be a saint. He couldn't do it. He tried his best, but his best was not enough. He accepted his human nature. "I know that nothing good lives in me, that is, in my sinful nature. For I have the desire to do what is good, but I cannot carry it out. For what I do is not the good I want to do; no, the evil I do not want to do—this I keep on doing" (Romans 7:18-19). Don't "should" yourself to death. There are times in life when everyone decides to do what they want to do and not what they ought to do. Even the best of the saints will admit that openly.

Give yourself a break. Put yourself on parole. By now you have probably punished yourself (and others) enough. What good is it to you to keep fretting about this stuff? Is it worth a year or a month more of feeling guilty? Maybe you can drop it now.

At least do this much for yourself. Grow up. There is no sense in "applying a five-year-old morality to a thirty-five-year-old problem."[28] Continuing to kick yourself is childish behavior. Mature judgment will help you to understand your behavior and to evaluate it in a reasonable light.

Those days and nights of your past are dead and gone. The time has come to bury them. Guilt looks backward. No matter how much guilt and blame you are willing to accept, there's absolutely nothing you can do to change the facts of history. You can do better next time only if you eliminate the handicap of past times. They are not holding you. You are holding them. Let go. Now. We have come full circle. We end where we began. *If I am forgiven, why do I still feel guilty?* We noted in the beginning that time by itself heals nothing. In the pages that followed we saw that time could be used to take some healthy steps in the right direction. You have been assured that God loves you and forgives you. If you still feel guilty, it may be because it takes awhile for our feelings to catch up with our understanding.

"Blessed is he whose transgression is forgiven, whose sin is covered." *Psalm 32:1 KJV*

"I love the LORD, for he heard my voice; he heard my cry for mercy." *Psalm 116:1*

Let It Hit Home

☐ Are you uncomfortable laughing with those who laugh and weeping with those who weep? If so, why?

☐ Are you willing to move on with your life? What is there to stop you?

☐ Wherever you are right now, is there anything that can prevent you from accepting God's forgiveness?

Notes

1. Bruce D. Hutchison, *Psycho-Logic* (Englewood Cliffs, N.J.: Prentice-Hall, 1983), p. 17f.
2. Judi Culbertson & Patti Bard, *Games Christians Play* (New York: Harper & Row, 1967), p. 78f.
3. *Boston Globe*, 21 July 1983.
4. *Boston Globe*, 21 July 1983.
5. Ibid.
6. Paul Tournier, *Guilt and Grace* (San Francisco: Harper & Row Publishers, 1962), p. 194.
7. John Calvin, *Institutes of the Christian Religion*, vol. 1 (Grand Rapids: William B. Eerdmans Publishing Company, 1957), p. 543.
8. *The Book of Common Prayer* of the Episcopal Church, pp. 62-63.
9. Thomas Alvarez, *The Prayers of St. Teresa of Avila* (New York: New City Press, 1990), p. 8.
10. Murphy's Law Calendar (Price/Stern/Sloan Publishers, Inc. 1983).
11. John-Roger & Peter McWilliams, *Life 101* (Los Angeles: Prelude Press, 1991).

12. Bernard Bangley, translation of *Introduction to the Devout Life* in *Spiritual Treasure* (Ramsey, N.J.: Paulist Press, 1984).

13. Augustus M. Toplady, "Rock of Ages" in *The Hymnbook* (Richmond, Philadelphia, New York: Presbyterian Church in the United States, The United Presbyterian Church in the U.S.A., Reformed Church in America, 1955).

14. Christine Herbruck, *Breaking the Cycle of Child Abuse* (Minneapolis: Winston Press, 1979), p. 42.

15. *The Twelve Steps for Adult Children* (San Diego: Recovery Publications, 1987), p. 51.

16. Sister Lelia Makra, translation of *The Hsiao Ching* (New York: St. John's University Press, 1961), chapter XVIII.

17. Melvin Konner, *The Tangled Wing* (New York: Holt, Rinehart, and Winston, 1982).

18. David Winter, *Walking into Light: a reinterpretation of* The Confessions of Saint Augustine, in *Christian Classics in Modern English* (Wheaton, Ill.: Harold Shaw Publishers, 1991).

19. Bernard Bangley, *Growing in His Image: a reinterpretation of Thomas à Kempis'* The Imitation of Christ, in *Christian Classics in Modern English* (Wheaton, Ill.: Harold Shaw Publishers, 1991).

20. David Winter, *Closer Than A Brother: a reinterpretation of Brother Lawrence's,* The Practice of the Presence of God, in *Christian Classics in Modern English* (Wheaton, Ill.: Harold Shaw Publishers, 1991).

21. Thomas Kelly, *A Testament of Devotion* (Nashville: The Upper Room, 1955).

22. Calvin Miller, *The Singer; The Song;* and *The Finale* (Downers Grove, Ill.: InterVarsity Press, 1975, 1977, 1979).

23. Walter Wangerin, Jr., *Ragman and Other Cries of Faith* (San Francisco: Harper & Row Publisher, 1984).

24. Helen Bacovcin, *The Way of a Pilgrim* (Garden City, N.Y.: Doubleday Company, 1979).

25. John Baillie, *A Diary of Private Prayer* (New York: Charles Scribner's Sons, 1949).

26. John James & Frank Cherry, *The Grief Recovery Handbook* (New York: Harper & Row, 1988), p. 47f.

27. *Sarasota Herald-Tribune*, 8 October 1983, p. 1-D.

28. Bruce Hutchison, *Psycho-Logic* (Englewood Cliffs, N.J.: Prentice-Hall, 1983), p. 183.